PRAISE FOR HOW **HEAVEN INVADES** EARTH

Kris sounds a clear prophetic call to embrace change. Through-out the pages of this book he commissions us to make earth like heaven. You will receive an impartation of supernatural faith and courage as you journey through the pages of this book and become part of the Kingdom mandate to transform society.

Ché **Ahn**
Senior Pastor, Harvest Rock Church
President and Founder, Harvest International Ministry

Kris charges ahead with the spirit of Caleb and Joshua to say that God has given us the greatest opportunity ever to bring in His kingdom with power and love, integrity and victory. *How Heaven Invades Earth* will motivate new Christians, students, and old saints alike to shake off that which hinders, and run for God. I learned so much; I am reading this book again.

John **Arnott**
Toronto Airport Church

Our very good friend Kris Vallotton has written a positive, detailed vision of the church as an effective catalyst for world transformation through the demonstration of both power and love. He and his church have transformed our own family and ministry by genuine apostolic love and friendship, and we are so encouraged by this. Thought provoking, and controversial in places, he makes a strong case for the church to set out to improve the world rather than let the devil steal our future. This is our present mandate as Christians and leaders, even as we look forward to the last days when God will glorify Himself and bring back His Son in magnificent power and majesty.

Rolland and Heidi **Baker**
Founding Directors, Iris Ministries

Kris Vallotton lives what he writes. He is the revolutionary who puts fire in my bones. He is gifted to understand human relationships and the dynamics, which trigger revival. I am glad he is on our side. In this book he explains revelatory truth, but more importantly, he imparts fire. Don't just read this. Catch it!

Harold R. Eberle
Founder of Worldcast Ministries

How Heaven Invades Earth is a perspective of the spiritual world we live that is like seeing from Google Earth. It will draw the reader into Kris's core messages of the last couple years. He does a masterful job assembling a collage of snapshots that build a highway of revelation to what the Spirit is doing in this coming Apostolic Age. True to form, Kris will challenge you to think outside the lines as he introduces numerous new dynamics that are in play in this generation. Read this book with an expectation of transformation.

Danny Silk
Family Life Pastor at Bethel Church
Author of *Developing a Culture of Honor* and *Loving Our Kids on Purpose*

No one can read a work out of Bethel Church, Redding, California, without the awareness of the culture and atmosphere in which it was produced. I was recently privileged with the opportunity of spending a week around Bethel, its leaders, its people, its students and servants where the culture of honor is well known. You would be interested to know that my report is that it is real and universally atmospheric.

To know Kris Vallotton is to be acquainted with honor and to see and sense this atmosphere. Hard-hitting, direct and prophetic, but oh so gentle, the author of this book lives what he writes. If one is offended by what is written within these pages it is probably, in part, because of the lack of acquaintance with Kris himself. Another consideration for offense is dealing with entrenched traditions that are being hammered herein.

Honor is inseparable from favor, respect and acceptance. When one chooses honor, as has the whole Bethel team, these qualities are inevitable and real.

Yes, you will be challenged, shocked and, if open-minded, you will be beneficially stretched. Reading *How Heaven Invades Earth* will likely be similar to being in a pouring rain, a cold-water-in-your-face experience coupled with a blurred view of one's surroundings. But when the rain is over and the view clears, you will be different!

Jack Taylor
President, Dimensions Ministries
Melbourne, Florida

The Church, as most Americans think of it, may help some individuals but it cannot be a viable means to reform our society. Why? *How Heaven Invades Earth* is the most insightful book I have yet encountered to answer that question. The creative suggestions that Kris Vallotton makes for correcting our past weaknesses and reforming our churches are powerful, positive and productive. I want to be part of the exciting kind of church that I read about here, and I believe you will agree!

C. Peter Wagner
Founder and Chancellor Emeritus, Wagner Leadership Institute

KRIS VALLOTTON

HOW **HEAVEN** **INVADES** EARTH
Transform the World Around You

Regal

For more information and
special offers from Regal Books, email us at
subscribe@regalbooks.com

Published by Regal
From Gospel Light
Ventura, California, U.S.A.
www.regalbooks.com
Printed in the U.S.A.

Library of Congress Cataloging-in-Publication Data
Vallotton, Kris.
How heaven invades earth : transform the world around you / Kris Vallotton.
p. cm.
ISBN 978-0-8307-6644-4 (trade paper)
1. Church and the world. 2. Apostolate (Christian theology)
3. Church renewal—Pentecostal churches. I. Title.
BR115.W6V26 2010
262'.1—dc22
2010029911

Rights for publishing this book outside the U.S.A. or in non-English languages are
administered by Gospel Light Worldwide, an international not-for-profit ministry.
For additional information, please visit www.glww.org, email info@glww.org, or write
to Gospel Light Worldwide, 1957 Eastman Avenue, Ventura, CA 93003, U.S.A.

To order copies of this book and other Regal products in bulk quantities,
please contact us at 1-800-446-7735.

"And it shall be in the last days," God says,
"that I will pour forth of My Spirit on all mankind."

ACTS 2:17

I dedicate this book to my children's children's children's children. Though we won't meet until we get to heaven, I wanted you to know that I had you in mind as I wrote every word of this book, and I continue to hold you in my heart. You will become the answer to my prayers and fulfillment of my prophecies. By the time you read this book, I will be watching you from heaven (see Hebrews 12:1).

Contents

Foreword

The disciples expected Jesus to establish His earthly kingdom at any moment. They were counting on Him to take Israel back to the rightful place of influence it once had under kings David and Solomon. Cities and nations would then live in the fulfillment of a much-anticipated promise under the glorious reign of their Messiah. This thought captured so much of their attention that they were vying for top honors in His kingdom. There was a flaw in their thinking, and therefore in their expectations, so Jesus told them a story—a parable (see Luke 19:11-17).

He told them about a landowner who gave a mina (a sum of money) to each of his 10 servants. They were to invest that money and make a profit for their master so that upon his return he could gather his earnings. When the first servant came to him, he reported that the master's mina had earned him 10 more minas. Then the landowner did something very unusual. He told the servant he was now in charge of 10 cities. In one moment the faithful servant became a ruler.

This parable answered at least two of the issues the disciples hadn't seen clearly. The first was that they were looking for a *sudden event* to make Jesus ruler of cities and nations, but Jesus took them to the *process* of stewardship. Simply speaking, He taught them that correctly stewarding what God puts in our hands increases our influence over humanity—specifically cities. Second, it reveals how we get personal promotion: through faithfulness in whatever God assigns to us. Going from a servant to a governor is quite a promotion. And when that promotion brings the influence of the King of kings through that servant to a whole city, we see a practical manifestation of the Kingdom on earth.

This story reveals how simple the subject of the Kingdom can be. And that is the message of *How Heaven Invades Earth*. My dear friend and author Kris Vallotton has done a great job capturing the heart of God for the Church in these last days. You'll not find any charts, predictions about the antichrist, discussions on the tribulation or any of the other hot-button subjects. Instead, this is a book about heart, God's heart. And that discovery is what shapes our attitude, focus and priorities more than any other. That is what excites me about this book: Kris puts his attention on where we have responsibility, not where we have curiosity. His insights are consistent with the theme of the gospel that "whatever is not from faith is sin." We must be wary of any teaching of the last days that doesn't require faith to obtain what God promises.

We live at a time when it seems the evil of this world is becoming more pronounced, while the glory of God in the Church is also being put on display in more glorious and obvious manners. Dick Joyce, a prophet and dear friend of both Kris and mine, once shared a prophetic word with us that went something like this: "Just as a jeweler lays a piece of black velvet across the counter upon which to display his precious gems, so the Lord is using the darkness of world circumstances as the backdrop for His display of His glory in the church." For me, this word helps to settle the tension we face any time we discuss the subject of the last days—darkness and light, both increasing.

We must learn to be people of great hope, regardless of world circumstances. Jesus always has a victorious plan in place. It is up to us to discover and implement that plan. *How Heaven Invades Earth* is sure to play a significant role in releasing the people of God into their glorious role in these glorious days.

Bill Johnson, Senior Leader, Bethel Church
Author, *When Heaven Invades Earth* and *Face to Face with God*

Acknowledgments

Kathy: You are the woman of my dreams and my best friend. Thank you for believing in me when I failed so miserably and reminding me of who I am in God.

Mom: Thanks for loving me and supporting me my entire life.

Grandpa: You taught me how to be a man and loved me when my father died when I was three years old. Although you have gone on to be with the Lord, your life still lives on through me.

Jaime and Marty: I love you both so much. I am very proud that you are a part of my legacy. Your encouragement in my life has been invaluable. You are both world-class leaders.

Shannon and Cameron: I love you. You inspire me to believe God for the people whom others throw away. You have done such an amazing job of pastoring Mountain Chapel, the place this movement all started.

Jason: I love your wisdom in my life. Your insight into the Kingdom is nothing less than supernatural. Your strength has often encouraged me to press on in hard times. I love you, son.

Gene: You inspire all of us with your life. Your ability to overcome impossible obstacles gives me courage to touch others with God's love. I am proud of you, son.

Bill and Beni: Serving God with you has been a dream come true. Your example in my life and in the Body of Christ gave me the inspiration to write this book.

Bill Derryberry: Your life is an inspiration to me. Your love has brought me wholeness.

Danny, Dann, Charlie and Paul: You have helped to shape my life, my ideas and my destiny. I love you with my whole heart.

Bethel team: Wow! You are amazing! It is a privilege to serve with you all.

The Prayer

In the midst of the darkest epoch season in human history, Jesus Christ had the audacity to teach us a prayer so powerful that it defies human reason. His words, spoken against the intense backdrop of adversity, would be forever remembered as the Lord's Prayer. In the midst of Roman oppression, with the reign of the evil emperor Nero within a stone's throw of history, Jesus turned to His tattered brigade of spiritual warriors and said, "Pray that my Father's kingdom would come and His will be done on earth, as it is in heaven." Was this prayer a sort of a wish upon a star, intended to be prayed by billions, but only to be experienced by a few in some distant eternity? No, I don't think so! I think Jesus actually expected us to believe that when we are empowered by the Holy Spirit, we can pull heaven down to earth.

Yet the planet seems to be groaning under the intense pressure of impending doom. The average person today is exposed to more bad news in a week than someone a hundred years ago would have heard in a lifetime. Is the earth eroding, or is it evolving? Is global warming the beginning of the intense heat that will reduce our world to a hot rock spinning hopelessly through space? Will evil finally triumph over good, leaving terrorism to ravage the righteous, rape the innocent and pillage our children? Will some maniac dictator finally push the button and blow us into oblivion? These are the great questions of our time. These threats press against our very souls, demanding real answers. To compound this sense of urgency, the future of our children depends on us getting this right.

When Heaven Invades Earth

I think we can all agree that we will need a multitude of miracles to see the Lord's Prayer answered and our destiny fulfilled. In his best-selling book *When Heaven Invades Earth,* Bill Johnson calls the Body of Christ back to our supernatural roots. He challenges all Christians to walk in signs and wonders as Jesus so clearly outlined in the Bible, including Mark's Gospel:

> He who has believed and has been baptized shall be saved; but he who has disbelieved shall be condemned. These signs will accompany those who have believed: in My name they will cast out demons, they will speak with new tongues; they will pick up serpents, and if they drink any deadly poison, it will not hurt them; they will lay hands on the sick, and they will recover (Mark 16:16-18).

Jesus never meant for miracles to be an end in themselves, but rather an invitation into a superior Kingdom—a catalyst to cultural transformation fueled by revival. Jesus told the city of Capernaum, "If the miracles had occurred in Sodom which occurred in you, it would have remained to this day" (Matthew 11:23). To the cities of Chorazin and Bethsaida, He said, "If the miracles had occurred in Tyre and Sidon which occurred in you, they would have repented long ago in sackcloth and ashes" (Matthew 11:21). Our Lord's message is clear; the manifestation of miracles is meant to create a world in revival.

There are some people today who want to remind us that Jesus pronounced judgment over the three cities that didn't repent in the New Testament. I would like to point out a couple of things about the judgments of Jesus. First of all, the only cities Jesus rebuked were towns that had witnessed His incredible miracles. When people experience the supernatural manifestations of the kingdom of God—when, for instance, the dead are raised, the blind receive their sight, the lame walk, lepers are cleansed and people are delivered from demons—they witness two kingdoms in contrast. This juxtaposition provides them with an opportunity to repent. A Church that does not demonstrate the miraculous works of Christ has failed to give the world this opportunity, and thus has no right to judge people for their lack of response.

Without miracles, the kingdom of God is reduced to words, concepts and good works. Perceived through this paradigm, the Lions, Rotary and Moose clubs would be the ones contending for first place. These things are important, but it is imperative that we demonstrate the power of our great King so the distinction between darkness and light is obvious and the Lord's Prayer can be answered.

There is one other thing I want to highlight concerning the judgments of Christ. It makes sense that a miracle-working, sinless Savior who created the entire world, a Man who needs no mercy, can have strong feelings about the destiny of cities. On the other hand, people like us, who got into the Kingdom through the whipped skin of His back and His nail-scarred hands (and not by our own works), ought to be a little more patient with people who are still lost in darkness! You think?

More than Miracles

Miracles that would have transformed Sodom, Tyre and Sidon did take place in Capernaum, Chorazin and Bethsaida, and yet those cities were not transformed! Maybe that's why Jesus said, "He who believes in Me, the works that I do, he will do also; and greater works than these he will do; because I go to the Father" (John 14:12). Without believers demonstrating the miracles of

Jesus, the planet will continue to erode into gross darkness that defies explanation. The populace will be reduced to the cesspool of demonic works, leaving hopelessness to encompass the earth like a thick, black cloud.

It is true, therefore, that supernatural works are a major component to revival, but miracles alone don't always lead to city transformation, as Jesus articulated so well in the Gospels. So the question remains: *How* does heaven invade earth in a way that earth becomes like heaven? That is the subject of this book. May the Lord Himself meet you in the pages of this book and commission you to change the world.

1

Re-forming
the Church

*Bureaucracy is like setting up scaffolding around a house
to paint the place, and instead painting the scaffolding for
25 years until the house finally falls down.*

PAUL MANWARING

Our Field of Dreams

The Church is God's mandated agency for world transformation.
But the Body of Christ needs another reformation so that we can
be the source of life we were meant to be in this dark world of oppression. The reformation we need is described in the parable of
the two brothers who made different choices that led to the same
result—separation from their Father. For some of us, reformation
will come when we, like the prodigal son, leave the pig farm of
our wrong, impoverished thinking and are renewed by the Father's radical love. Only then can we shed the tattered rags of our
global orphanage and put on the powerful mantle of God's Royal
Family. Our heavenly Father waits expectantly in our field of
dreams, ready to restore us with His *robe of identity*, empower us
with His *ring of authority* and give us His understanding with the
sandals of purity. These thongs separate us from the defilement of
worldly thinking and ensure our true eternal inheritance.

Meanwhile, back at the ranch, many of us, like the prodigal's elder brother, have forgotten how to celebrate, have lost sight of our own inheritance and have replaced sonship with sacrifice and servanthood. Sacrifice and servanthood are important Kingdom attributes as long as they embrace and don't replace family values. If the Church is going to be the tipping point of historic exploits, then we must identify old religious paradigms that are hindering the coming Kingdom and then reposition ourselves alongside the Father to welcome the harvest home. This is a dramatic paradigm shift from the Church in which most of us were raised, but it is being fueled by a changing epoch season in the kingdom of heaven itself. Let me explain.

**Or heavenly Father waits expectantly
in our field of dreams.**

Moving from Denominationalism to Apostleships

In 1998, my wife, Kathy, and I moved to Redding, California, to launch the Bethel School of Supernatural Ministry. That same year, I was lying on the floor praying one morning when the Lord spoke to me so clearly that it stunned me. He said, "There is a new epoch season emerging in this hour. Much like the Protestant Reformation, there is another reformation coming that will unearth the very foundation of Christianity. This move of the Spirit will absolutely redefine your ideologies and philosophies concerning what the Church is and how she should function."

I asked Him, "What will this transition look like?"

He said, "My Church is moving from denominationalism to apostleships."

I actually had no idea what He was talking about, so I asked Him what the difference was between denominationalism and apostleships. He explained to me that in denominationalism, believers gather around doctrinal agreement and divide when they disagree. In apostleships, believers rally around fathers, mothers and families. He said, "I am about to open up the vaults of heaven and reveal depths of My glory that have never before been seen or understood by any living creature." He explained that this glory was going to be revealed to and through His Church in what can only be called a new epoch season. Then He stated, "If I pour out new revelation into the wineskin of denominationalism, it will rip the wineskin and the wine will be lost" (see Luke 5:37-39).

The Lord used the term "denominational*ism*" and not "denominations." "Ism" often denotes a distnct ideology, as in communism, racism or humanism. These ideologies are built upon distortions of the truth. They are lies sponsored by a diabolical agenda, creating oppression wherever these ideas gain influence. I am personally convinced the "ism" of denominationalism is an evil spirit! It is every bit as alive in nondenominational churches and some apostolic networks as it is in denominational churches.

We were named Protestants because we were born in a doctrinal protest.

It's easy to see that denominations have grown up through division, being rooted in the Protestant Reformation of the sixteenth century. We were named Protestants because we were born in a doctrinal protest (the word originally meant "pro-testament" but soon took on the meaning *protester*), which continues to this day.

Both the Protestant Reformation and the movements that have sprung up from it emphasize doctrinal agreement above relationship. This priority has created a culture that constantly threatens to divide people at the very core of their bonding point. While many believers admit that damaged relationships and church splits are costly, the denominational mindset leads them to conclude that the way to avoid this is simply to find ways to enforce doctrinal conformity so disagreements can't arise. Thus, denominationalism also creates a culture that is critical of anyone who thinks outside the box of tradition, and it desperately fears inspiration.

Leaders under this spirit have more faith in the devil's power to deceive believers than the Holy Spirit's ability to lead them into all truth. Shepherds in denominationalism resist revelatory thinking because they understand that new ideas spawn disagreements and disagreement attacks the central nervous system of their churches.

I often refer to *denominationalism* as "divided nations," in reference to the way this spirit has infected and limited our ability to disciple the nations. We are called to disciple nations, not to divide people. Note that what I am emphasizing here are the complexities of doctrinal agreement, not the core tenets of faith. The five basic tenets include (1) the Trinity (Father, Son and Holy Spirit); (2) the person of Jesus Christ (who was born of a virgin, died for our sins, was resurrected and ascended into heaven) as true God and true man; (3) Jesus' visible return for His Bride; (4) our salvation by grace through faith in Christ; and (5) the inerrant and authoritative nature of Scripture.

I further agree with Bethel Church's statement of faith.[1] Churches don't usually split over these fundamentals. Differences and division most often come over issues such as water baptism, speaking in tongues, the nature of leadership, eschatology, money, power, attire and the like.

The Catholic Church

We can gain some great insight by contrasting the Protestant movement with the Catholic Church, who is mother of the Protestant Church. In fact, let's do a little trivia: How many times has the Catholic Church split in the last 2,000 years? The right answer is *three times*! How many times has the Protestant Church split since the Reformation? Okay, I will make the question easier: How many times has the Protestant Church split this month? Okay, one more question: What does the Catholic Church call the leaders of their local churches? The right answer is *father*! Are you gaining any insight yet? The apostle Paul put it this way: "For if you were to have countless tutors in Christ, yet you would not have many fathers, for in Christ Jesus I became your father through the gospel" (1 Corinthians 4:15).

In the 1960s, the Catholic priests preached their messages in Latin! I think it's pretty easy to see that Catholics didn't come to church to hear a great message, because many of them probably didn't even understand the language. As Protestants, we understand the disadvantages of not preaching the Word, and I appreciate that. But why do Catholics go to church? I would like to propose to you that they don't gather because they agree but because they are loyal to a family.

Is it possible that when Protestants protested bad doctrine at the price of relationship, we came under another curse just as destructive? (Something to think about.)

Processing Conflict

All of us speak with an accent, though we often don't realize it until we are in the presence of someone who speaks with an accent that is different from ours (and, of course, we all tend to think it's the other person who has the accent). What most of us don't realize is that we also *see* with an accent. This visual accent is a kind of processing prejudice—a lens—that shapes our view of the world, of the Kingdom and of the Bible by causing us to see things not *as they are* but *as we believe they are*. Thus, as we live out our faith and read the Bible, we look for and expect to see that which validates what we already believe. In other words, we tend to see only what we are *prepared* to see.

Dr. Lance Wallnau, a respected author and teacher, drove this point home for me at a conference recently. He brought a barrel of varicolored flags up on stage and gave us 30 seconds to count all the gold flags. Then he instructed us to close our eyes and asked us how many red flags were in the container. Of course, no one could answer the question, because we had only counted the gold flags. This is such a great picture of our tendency to read our own core values, life experiences and doctrinal prejudices into what the Bible says. The danger is that we sometimes make the Bible say something it doesn't say by selective seeing.

The lens of denominationalism is primarily defined by the priority of doctrinal agreement, which necessitates a negative view of disagreement in the Body of Christ. Therefore, when someone with a denominational lens approaches Scripture, it requires that biblical terms and concepts support the goal of eliminating disagreement, and ultimately, discouraging individualism.

For example, we can see this in the denominational approach to terms like "loyalty" and "unity." In denominationalism, loyalty is often redefined as "agreeing with the leader." Disagreement is called "disloyalty," and often "disrespect." But the truth is that loyalty is actually only tested when we don't agree. For example, David's loyalty to King Saul was revealed not when he lived in the king's house as his favored son-in-law, but when he lived in the wilderness as the king's hated and hunted rival. If we agree with our leader over an issue, then we are going to do what our leader wants us to do anyway, *because* we agree. It is only when we disagree that the fabric of our relationship is put to the test.

Unity of the Spirit

The *unity of the Spirit* is another great example of a powerful truth that has been reduced to mean that "we should all agree on everything so the world will believe there really is a God." Viewing the Bible through the lens of denominationalism redefines the *unity of the Spirit* to mean the *unity of understanding and agreeing upon the Word.*

Let's consider one of the premier passages of Scripture on unity—the prayer of Jesus recorded in John 17:

> As You sent Me into the world, I also have sent them into the world. For their sakes I sanctify Myself, that they themselves also may be sanctified in truth. I do not ask on behalf of these alone, but for those also who believe in Me through their word; *that they may all be one; even as You, Father, are in Me and I in You, that they also may be in Us,* so that the world may believe that You sent Me. The glory which You have given Me I have given to them, that they may be one, just as We are one; I in them and You in Me, that they may be perfected in unity, so that the world may know that You sent Me, and loved them, even as You have loved Me (John 17:18-23, emphasis added).

I have heard many messages on unity in which this passage is used to exhort believers to get along. But did you notice that, contrary to popular opinion, the unity that Jesus prayed for in this passage is not the unity between believers but unity between a believer and God? Look closely at His prayer. Jesus petitioned the

Father "that they may all be one; even as You, Father, are in Me and I in You, that *they also may be in Us.*" It is easy to assume that "all be one" refers to being one with each other; but Jesus defines it as being one with God. Okay, now look at the next verse: "Just as We are one; *I in them* and You in Me, that they may be perfected in unity." Again, the key emphasis here is "I in them." Nowhere does Jesus pray that we should be "in" each other!

It doesn't seem to occur to most of us that Jesus couldn't even get His 12 disciples to get along with each other when He walked the earth with them. But when we read these verses with denominational mindsets, we need Jesus to be praying against disagreements, because these days, disagreement equals church splits. In doing so, we miss one of the most powerful truths in the Bible. God wants to be one with His people! The prayer that Jesus prayed in John 17 is actually an extension of the talk He had earlier with His disciples in John 14. Let's check it out:

> He who has seen Me has seen the Father; how can you say, "Show us the Father"? Do you not believe that I am in the Father, and the Father is in Me? The words that I say to you I do not speak on My own initiative, but the Father abiding in Me does His works. Believe Me that I am in the Father and the Father is in Me; otherwise believe because of the works themselves. Truly, truly, I say to you, he who believes in Me, the works that I do, he will do also; and greater works than these he will do; because I go to the Father (John 14:9-12).

Jesus told His guys, "If you have seen me, you have seen the Father." We know for a fact that Jesus was not saying that He is the Father, because a voice from heaven said, "This is my beloved Son, in whom I am well-pleased" when He was baptized

(Matthew 3:17). Jesus wasn't talking to Himself! Jesus was simply making the point that He and the Father are an inseparable unity. For example, if you mix red paint and blue paint, you get the color purple. Every time you see purple, you know it is the manifestation of these two primary colors. But I defy you to separate them once they are mixed. The Father and the Son are the manifestation of a celestial union that transcends human rationalization or finite explanation.

Jesus said the works (miracles) He did were signs of the Father's presence working through Him. This tells us that, while we may not be able to *explain* the nature of this union, we can *experience* it. But wait, it gets even better. Jesus shocks us with this next decree: "He who believes in Me, the works that I do, he will do also; and greater works than these he will do" (John 14:12). Okay, now let's put this all together. Jesus prayed in John 17 that the Body of Christ would be united with the Godhead in the same way that He is united with His Father. The implication is that when people *see us, they have seen the Father!* And therefore, if they don't believe us on account of our words, they should believe us on account of our works, because we are to do greater works than Jesus did! Now that is the kind of unity that will cause the world to know that the kingdom of God has come near them!

The implication is that when people see us, they have seen the Father!

Apostolic Paradigm Shifts

In apostleships, the priority of relationships is kept above full doctrinal agreement, promoting highly relational core connections.

Apostles create *covenantal, family* relationships, because believers are attached to and through *fathers and family*, not doctrine. This promotes freedom for people to think creatively, to dream, to envision with God and to experience new depths of the Holy Spirit. This relational security creates an environment that attracts revelation. The very nature of revelation is that people get fresh perspectives and deeper insights from God's Word *and* have extraordinary encounters with the supernatural kingdom of God.

Disagreement does exist in apostolic cultures; in fact, you could say that the culture even encourages it, or certainly allows it, by inviting revelation. Doctrinal disputes often arise as believers process fresh truth that frequently assails old, traditional mindsets. The challenge in an apostolic culture is to maintain strong, respectful and loving connections with one another as we work through these revelatory insights.

Revelation has always been the child of relationship more than it is the fruit of intense study. Jesus put it this way: "No longer do I call you slaves, for the slave does not know what his master is doing; but I have called you friends, for all things that I have heard from My Father I have made known to you" (John 15:15). Relating to God as a slave keeps us in the dark ages when it comes to understanding the Father's business. But friendship with God unlocks the heavenly vault of His secrets, exposing treasures that have been hidden in Him from eternity.

Moses indicated that revelation belongs to a relational context when he wrote, "The secret things belong to the LORD our God, but the things revealed belong to us and to our sons forever" (Deuteronomy 29:29). When God reveals His Kingdom secrets to us, they become part of our ancestral dynasty, which is to be passed down from generation to generation, much like a family business or a plot of land. Doctrinal insights were meant to be carried relationally, not discovered in the think tanks of denominational seminaries. We see this in the life of Joshua, who received wisdom from fatherly impartation when Moses laid his hands on him rather than require of him laborious study or years of experience. Deuteronomy 34:9 says, "Now Joshua the son of Nun was filled with the spirit of wisdom, for Moses had laid his hands on him."

About the Father's Business

I am not saying that doctrinal agreement isn't important in the Church. It is important, but it simply does not hold the place of primacy. I like to illustrate the importance of correctly ordering our priorities by looking at the product sales industry, in which two of the main divisions of the business have competing core values. There is the manufacturing division, which typically has a "zero defect" core value, and there is the research and development division, which has a "discovery by trial and error" core value.

For example, when Apple Corporation went to market with their first iPhone, the goal of the manufacturing department was to have no defects whatsoever in the phones they were selling. But the research and development department, which invented the iPhone, probably made hundreds of mistakes in the process of developing the product. If Apple tried to apply the same core values to the R&D department as it did to the manufacturing division, they would never invent any products. This would eventually result in Apple having nothing to bring to market, and soon they would be forced into bankruptcy. In other words, even though both of these divisions are part of the same great company, success in these two departments is measured much differently. Mistakes are the inevitable process of invention, but they are the demise of production.

The priority of agreement in denominationalism creates a "no defects" policy that makes little to no room for the discovery process that empowers innovation, invention and revelation. When truth isn't processed perfectly the first time, the entire revelation is usually discarded as "heresy" or maligned as "dangerous." A branch of Christianity called the Shepherding Movement is a great example of this. This movement was birthed through some incredible revelation and insights into fatherhood, discipleship, authority and accountability. But many among the leadership of this movement used these truths to control instead of to empower believers. Therefore, the larger Church threw out the entire revelation as unbiblical, which has greatly hindered progress in these important areas.

Two other cases in point are the Latter Day Rain and the Manifest Sons of God movements. Christians who were a part of these movements had some real insights into the true identity of believers. But many of the leaders of the movements began to use their insights to promote spiritual elitism, and the entire revelation was branded as heretical.

The "no defects" policy of denominationalism is a problem, for one, because we are applying it to the wrong area. Our individual character and our relationship with God and man are the things that belong in the "manufacturing department," so to speak. These are the areas in which we should strive for zero defects. The R&D departments of the Church include learning to apply truth, digging deeper into the Word, experimenting with the Holy Spirit, moving in the gifts, stepping out in faith, dreaming with God, attempting the impossible, believing the unreasonable, and so on. Of course, both departments exist in the same people, so the illustration breaks down a bit here.

In reality, we must learn to balance the priorities of risk-taking and excellence in all areas of life—in our character development, our relationships and in our pursuit of revelation. The problem is that risk-taking creates messes, exposes flaws and, more often than not, teaches us what *doesn't work*. But this is the process that leads to true spiritual maturity. It is essential that the Body of Christ develop and embrace an attitude of risk, or soon we will be eating old, worm-infested manna. If we are to be the light of the world, then we must start emanating who God is through cutting-edge Kingdom insights and stop reflecting the world's outdated, stale philosophies and strategies that, for the most part, are simply repackaged traditional mindsets. God is the same yesterday, today and forever (see Heb. 13:8), but what He is doing in the world isn't static. He is always moving forward.

Apostleships value the call of the wild over the circus, choosing to risk their lives in the natural habitat of the kingdom of heaven rather than be a tourist in the artificial environment of the spiritual zoo.

Apostleships value the call of the wild over the circus.

The Kingdom Always Lies at Risk

When we look closely at the beginning of creation, we see that God Himself is a risk-taker. He didn't childproof the Garden; instead, He planted two trees there: the Tree of Life and the Tree of Knowledge of Good and Evil. The latter would kill a man within 24 hours of eating its fruit (see Genesis 2:17). God gave man the chance to live forever, but only at the risk of the death penalty.

Let's look at another great example of the risky life of the Kingdom. Jesus went to a wedding party with His 12 guys and

His mother. After they had partied for a long time, they ran out of wine. Mary pressed her Son into making more wine. (I always wonder how Mary knew Jesus could make wine, unless He was doing miracles at home.) John records the incident in his Gospel:

> When the headwaiter tasted the water which had become wine, and did not know where it came from (but the servants who had drawn the water knew), the headwaiter called the bridegroom, and said to him, "Every man serves the good wine first, and when the people have drunk freely, then he serves the poorer wine; but you have kept the good wine until now" (John 2:9-10).

The words "drunk freely" in this passage is the Greek word *methuo*. It means to be drunk or intoxicated. Jesus made wine for people who were already drunk! God was not condoning drunkenness! There is no way the Lord wanted people to get drunk—the Bible makes that clear in several other passages (see Ephesians 5:18; Galatians 5:21). But God doesn't control people. In fact, He actually provides options and then empowers people to make great choices. When we make the right choices, He rewards us. If God were to take away our bad choices, He would remove the possibility of a reward.

Denominationalism produces cultural sanitization by eliminating choices through religious control. Shepherds in this culture are charged with teaching people *what* to think, not *how* to think. When people exercise their power to choose, whatever is inside of them—be it good, bad or ugly—has an opportunity to manifest. Most denominational cultures are simply unequipped to help people face the reality of who they are and empower them to take responsibility for their messes without controlling them.

Apostles, on the other hand, value risk because they understand that faith requires risk. Only a culture driven by risk-taking faith can produce life. Consequently, a high level of freedom exists in apostolic meetings and cultures, allowing believers to be extremely powerful or sadly pitiful. In order to preserve this freedom, apostolic cultures develop strategic, empowering ways to help people take responsibility for their choices and clean up their messes. (We will talk more about this later in the book.)

I have always found it easy to identify people who grow up in denominationalism, because they refuse to think for themselves. They are accustomed to their leaders doing all their thinking for them. I experienced this a couple of years ago in our School of Supernatural Ministry. We had just begun the school year, and I was teaching a fresh group of a couple hundred students. As I shared, I allowed the students to ask questions. I was exhorting the students that day to take risks in God and not worry about failing.

A young man raised his hand and asked, "You are not talking about moral failure are you?"

"Of course not," I responded.

I continued teaching, and a few minutes later his hand went up again.

"Johnny, do you have another question?"

"Yes," he said, looking like a lost puppy dog. "You are not saying that we should do things like jump off a roof by faith and see if God will catch us, are you?"

"No!" I said, a little impatient this time. "And I am not trying to convince you to drink poisoned Kool-Aid or wait for flying saucers either!"

Johnny went on to ask about five more questions in that session, all of them in the same vein. With every question, I grew more frustrated. (I used to say that there is no such thing as a stupid question. Johnny convinced me that I was wrong about that.)

Finally, in complete exasperation, I paused and said, "Okay, everyone. Ready? Turn on your brains! You have permission to think! If I say something that can be taken five different ways, please process it in the only way that makes sense as a Christian."

As the months passed, I got to know Johnny better. I discovered that he was brought up in a Christian home where his parents did all the thinking for him. To make matters worse, he was part of a church in which the pastor taught with the assumption that his people were stupid. This leader would painstakingly and methodically explain each of his points, closing all the wrong theological and philosophical doors, as if the room were filled with complete idiots. Consequently, Johnny's mind was reduced to memorizing and repeating facts. He had never learned how to process information or think for himself. The fear of being wrong had imprisoned his intellect and crushed his imagination.

Turn on your brains! You have permission to think!

Leaders in denominationalism tend to preach to convince people of truth. They seem to be under the impression that it is their responsibility to persuade people what to believe. Leaders in apostleships preach to inspire and encourage their people, understanding that while they are responsible to preach the Bible, it is the Holy Spirit's responsibility to lead people into all truth (see John 16:13). Apostolic leaders prize the relationship that believers have with the Holy Spirit. They train people to be dependent on the Holy Spirit because, ultimately, He is the one who is responsible for their maturity in Christ.

Relating to the Word

The goal of the Bible has always been to bring us into an encounter and relationship with God (see John 17:3). If knowing the Word and knowing God were synonymous, then the scribes and Pharisees, who memorized the entire Old Testament, would have been the first people to recognize and receive Christ. But their very approach to the Scriptures set them up for spiritual blindness. They abandoned the true purpose for studying the Word by exchanging a relationship with God for academic arguments, and never demanded that their theology lead to an encounter.

The goal of the Bible has always been to bring us into an encounter and relationship with God.

Someone might argue that if you base your relationship with God on an experience, you could be deceived. That is so true! But on the other hand, if you study the Bible and it doesn't lead you into an encounter with the Almighty, then you are already deceived! The moment theologians, or anybody else for that matter, abandon relationship with God as the *primary* mission in understanding the Bible, they have already begun to enter into deception. Paul described these people best when writing to Timothy. He said they have a "form of godliness, although they have denied its power" and are "always learning and never able to come to the knowledge of the truth" (2 Timothy 3:5,7).

In a sense, the Bible is somewhat like the owner's manual in a new car. You read the manual expecting to understand how to operate and take care of your automobile. If you memorize the manual and still can't operate the car, what purpose would there be in reading the manual? Often when you read the owner's manual you still don't quite understand how a certain feature functions until you try it out with the manual in hand. Can you imagine what the owner's manual would be like if the author of the manual had lost sight of that goal?

If you study the Bible and it doesn't lead you into an encounter with the Almighty, then you are already deceived!

In an apostolic culture, deception is primarily dealt with through relational accountability and spiritual discernment rather than intellectualism. For example, when the apostles in the Early Church struggled over doctrinal issues, they compared their understanding of the Scriptures with their experience in God in order to come to their conclusions about the truth. Let's look at one example in the book of Acts:

> Some of the sect of the Pharisees who had believed stood up, saying, "It is necessary to circumcise them and to direct them to observe the Law of Moses." The apostles and the elders came together to look into this matter. After there had been much debate, Peter stood up and said to them, "Brethren, you know that in the early days God made a choice among you, that by my mouth the Gentiles would hear the word of the gospel and believe. And God, who knows the heart, testified to them giving them the Holy Spirit, just as He also did to us; and He made no distinction between us and them,

cleansing their hearts by faith. Now therefore why do you put God to the test by placing upon the neck of the disciples a yoke which neither our fathers nor we have been able to bear? But we believe that we are saved through the grace of the Lord Jesus, in the same way as they also are." All the people kept silent, and they were listening to Barnabas and Paul as they were relating what signs and wonders God had done through them among the Gentiles. After they had stopped speaking, James answered, saying, "Brethren, listen to me. Simeon has related how God first concerned Himself about taking from among the Gentiles a people for His name. With this the words of the Prophets agree, just as it is written, "AFTER THESE THINGS I will return, AND I WILL REBUILD THE TABERNACLE OF DAVID WHICH HAS FALLEN, AND I WILL REBUILD ITS RUINS, AND I WILL RESTORE IT, SO THAT THE REST OF MANKIND MAY SEEK THE LORD, AND ALL THE GENTILES WHO ARE CALLED BY MY NAME," SAYS THE LORD, WHO MAKES THESE THINGS KNOWN FROM LONG AGO. Therefore it is my judgment that we do not trouble those who are turning to God from among the Gentiles, but that we write to them that they abstain from things contaminated by idols and from fornication and from what is strangled and from blood (Acts 15:5-20).

Notice that the apostles took Peter's experience with the Gentiles, the testimonies of Paul and Barnabas's signs and wonders into the debate to determine what their doctrinal stance should be concerning how the Law applied to the Gentiles. Apostleships most often value the voice of the Holy Spirit (see Acts 15:28) and God-experiences above academic arguments. They also tend to process first from their hearts rather than from their heads. I don't mean at all to communicate that apostleships are intellectually shallow or mindlessly motivated. I am simply pointing out that the Spirit directs apostles and, therefore, they often find themselves living beyond the boundaries of human logic and reason (not, of course, outside the counsel of the Scriptures).

A disciple following an apostolic leadership team will be required to exercise a high level of faith and trust as well as extreme discernment, because the structures, strategies, vision and mission of apostleships tend to be Spirit-inspired. By their very nature, apostles don't give *preeminence* to "common sense." Among many of my associates, this process of innovation in the working out of various aspects of an apostolic mission is termed "spirategies," meaning "Spirit-led strategies."

Resistance in some leaders to experience the impossible interventions of God has resulted in many believers being educated out of obedience.

Of course, this way of approaching life in the Kingdom is not new. It's demonstrated throughout the entire Bible. From Gideon's army of 300 pitcher-carrying soldiers, to Elisha's floating axe head, to Joshua's seven-day march around an enemy city, the Word of God is filled with irrational stories that defy common reason. Church leaders who have denominational mindsets often share these stories as awesome historic events of the God who does the unreasonable, the irrational and the impossible. But it never occurs to some of them that He still requires His people to trust Him to live a life that transcends our understanding, and invites us into His miraculous interventions.

This resistance in some leaders to experience the impossible interventions of God has resulted in many believers being educated out of obedience. They exchange God's works for good deeds, reducing "Jesus people" to only being nice, friendly citizens instead of fire-breathing world changers. They have domesticated the Lion of the tribe of Judah, reducing Him to a circus animal.

Transitioning from a Hierarchy to a Heir-archy

The move from denominationalism to apostleships will create an organic metamorphosis where the Body of Christ transitions from denominational slavery to being what they should be—joint-heirs with Christ. Let me begin to explain this by highlighting a portion of Paul's letter to the Romans:

> For all who are being led by the Spirit of God, these are sons of God. For you have not received a spirit of slavery leading to fear again, but you have received a spirit of adoption as sons by which we cry out, "Abba! Father!" The Spirit Himself testifies with our spirit that we are children of God, and if children, heirs also, heirs of God and fellow heirs with Christ, if indeed we suffer with Him so that we may also be glorified with Him (Romans 8:14-17).

Paul points out that we are no longer slaves but adopted sons in which we now relate to God as our Daddy (the Aramaic word *Abba*)! Because our heavenly Father is also the King of the world, we, through inheritance, are heirs of the throne. It is important for us to understand that we received this promotion through adoption and not on the basis of our abilities. The ramifications of this royal nepotistic transition is that we are moving from a hierarchical leadership model to a heir-archy, as we are heirs with Christ to the throne of God (see Rev. 3:21).

Denominationalism is based on hierarchies. Hierarchies are most often developed through a pecking order. In a hen house, chickens organize their society by pecking each other in order to determine the top chicken, the bottom chicken and all the chickens in between. In other words, hierarchies are structures determined by the level of dominance a chicken has in the hen house, or in this case, a person has in an organization.

Denominationalism is a highly developed hen house where leaders receive authority by their performance. They go to a seminary, get a degree and become a pastor. The trouble with achievement-based authority is that it creates a performance-driven leadership culture where the most accomplished person is commissioned to lead. (There is nothing wrong with education or seminaries as long as they are not the ultimate qualifiers for leadership.) Because this type of leadership is primarily derived through works, anybody who outperforms his or her leader is a threat to the organization. Therefore, the culture itself is either subconsciously or proactively designed to undermine or sabotage (peck) anyone who is more accomplished than the leader. In this way, the leader's floor becomes the follower's ceiling.

Denominationalism is a highly developed hen house where leaders receive authority by their performance.

On the other hand, apostleships are heir-archies. In heir-archies, leaders are not determined by their ability to perform but by the level of favor they have received from God (Daddy) through their relationship with Him as a son or daughter. In other words, apostolic leaders receive authority not by *what* they know, but by *whom* they know. This is "called"-based leadership. Jesus, for example, *called* each of His disciples without regard to their educational qualifications or ministry experience. Here is the passage where the Lord enlisted the "Sons of Thunder," as He affectionately called them:

> Going on from there He saw two other brothers, James the son of Zebedee, and John his brother, in the boat with Zebedee their father, mending their nets; and He called them (Matthew 4:21).

Even the apostle Paul, who was extremely well educated and a highly qualified religious leader, said that God called him by His "grace." The Bible describes grace as the unmerited favor of God toward people. The key word here is "unmerited":

> But when God, who had set me apart even from my mother's womb and called me through His grace, was pleased to reveal His Son in me so that I might preach Him among the Gentiles, I did not immediately consult with flesh and blood, nor did I go up to Jerusalem to those who were apostles before me; but I went away to Arabia, and returned once more to Damascus (Galatians 1:15-17).

Leaders in apostleships are not necessarily uneducated, inexperienced or weak, but they are not put into leadership primarily because of their qualifications or their pedigree. Instead, they are installed as leaders because God chooses them. When God calls a person to lead, He releases favor on them. His favor qualifies them. There is a great illustration of this in the commissioning of Joshua:

> So the LORD said to Moses, "Take Joshua the son of Nun, a man in whom is the Spirit, and lay your hand on him; and have him stand before Eleazar the priest and before all the congregation, and commission him in their sight. You shall put some of your authority on him, in order that all the congregation of the sons of Israel may obey him" (Numbers 27:18-20).

True God-appointed leaders carry a certain majesty, splendor or favor about them.

We know that Joshua was the most qualified person to take Moses' place because he had served as his second-in-command for years. But God didn't mention Joshua's experience. Instead He reminded Moses that Joshua had the "Spirit" on him. The Spirit qualified Joshua to lead His people. God then instructed Moses to lay his hands on him and give him some of his authority. The Hebrew word for "authority" here is also translated "splendor" nine times, "majesty" six times and "beauty" or "glory" twice. True God-appointed leaders carry a certain majesty, splendor or favor about them that causes people to recognize their authority and want to follow them.

Mantles and Missions

When God commissions His leaders, like Joshua, He releases *mantles* over them. These *mantles* give them the supernatural ability to complete their mission. Unlike the gifts and calls of God that remain on a person for life, a *mantle* stays with the *mission,* not with the man. For example, anyone who becomes president of the United States has to be a very gifted person. A person doesn't rise to the highest office in our land without those qualifications. But on the day of the inauguration, something powerful takes place in the spirit realm; a presidential *mantle* from heaven is given to that person. God never grants someone an assignment without giving him or her the ability to complete it. God Himself establishes all authority in the universe, and therefore every leadership role on the planet is a mission from God (see Romans 13:1). The presidential *mantle* gives these leaders the capacity to direct our country beyond their human ability. However, when their term is over and they leave the White House, the *mantle* stays with the *mission* so it can be passed on to the next president. But their leadership *gifts* and *calling* remain with them.

Before Joshua ever received his own mantle, he had the chance to experience the effects of the mantle that rested on the shoulders of Moses. One of the most striking examples of this is found in Exodus 17, the story of Joshua being commissioned by Moses to take his soldiers and go down in the valley to fight Amalek. During the battle, Moses went up on the mountain and held up his hands. When Moses got tired and dropped his arms, Joshua began to lose the battle. When Moses lifted up his arms, Joshua won. It became clear to the Israelite leadership that Joshua's victory was directly related to Moses raising his hands, so they put a leader on each side of Moses to help support his arms until Joshua won the battle and defeated Amalek (see Exodus 17:8-13).

If we don't understand how to recognize and align ourselves under true spiritual authority, we may build bigger armies, develop better strategies and buy more powerful weapons, but we will still lose! It just never occurs to us that if we support (honor) our leaders, we will inherit their victories. But this is how leadership is designed to work in an apostleship. In an apostleship, honor between the leaders and those who follow creates a relationship in which the leaders' ceiling becomes the followers' floor.

**If we support (honor) our leaders,
we will inherit their victories.**

Angelic Help

The book of Revelation gives us some great insights into the way apostolic authority functions in the invisible realm. Jesus said to the apostle John:

> To the angel of the church in Ephesus write: The One who holds the seven stars in His right hand, the One who walks among the seven golden lampstands, says this: "I know your deeds and your toil and perseverance, and that you cannot tolerate evil men, and you put to the test those who call themselves apostles, and they are not, and you found them to be false; and you have perseverance and have endured for My name's sake, and have not grown weary. But I have this against you, that you have left your first love. Therefore remember from where you have fallen, and repent and do the deeds you did at first; or else I am coming to you and will remove your lampstand out of its place—unless you repent" (Revelation 2:1-5).

Notice that Jesus commissioned John to write seven letters that became the apostolic mandates for seven different churches throughout Asia. But did you catch the fact that John was not told to write the letters to the natural leaders of those churches? Instead, he was instructed to write the letters to the seven angels of the seven churches! *Wow!* What we learn from this passage is astonishing; we see that true apostolic ministries have angels assigned to them. These angels are commissioned to carry out the mission dictated by a particular apostle's mandate and *metron*. The word *metron* means the realm or boundaries of a leader's spiritual influence (see Romans 12:3; 2 Corinthians 10:13). In this case, John had authority over seven specific geographic regions, and so he had seven angels assigned to him.

It is my personal conviction that one of the essential elements that has mandated this apostolic age is that the angels no longer recognize the performance-based authority of denominationalism. Paul teaches us that angels recognize true spiritual authority and that this is essential for our prayers to be answered and our prophecies to be fulfilled (see 1 Corinthians 11:4,10). Angels are mentioned more than 180 times in the New Testament alone. Where have all the angels gone in the twenty-first-century Church? Isn't it possible that it was the angels who helped Joshua in the battle against the Amalekites (see Exodus 17:8-13)? What would the world be like if we were to suddenly employ angelic help on this planet in the same degree as they did in the first century? I think we are about to find out, as we are re-formed into this new apostolic wineskin.

Apostolic Covering

The apostle Paul was sent out by the apostles at Jerusalem and commissioned by the Holy Spirit (see Acts 15:22-25).

Subsequently, his ministry witnessed the effectiveness of covering that comes from submission to true spiritual authority. The difference between people who are under authority and those who aren't is evident in the contrast seen between Sceva's sons and Paul's ministry. The demonic realm didn't even recognize the authority of the sons of Sceva. Let's investigate the situation:

> God was performing extraordinary miracles by the hands of Paul, so that handkerchiefs or aprons were even carried from his body to the sick, and the diseases left them and the evil spirits went out. But also some of the Jewish exorcists, who went from place to place, attempted to name over those who had the evil spirits the name of the Lord Jesus, saying, "I adjure you by Jesus whom Paul preaches." Seven sons of one Sceva, a Jewish chief priest, were doing this. And the evil spirit answered and said to them, "I recognize Jesus, and I know about Paul, but who are you?" And the man, in whom was the evil spirit, leaped on them and subdued all of them and overpowered them, so that they fled out of that house naked and wounded (Acts 19:11-16).

It's amazing that an apostle's hankie had more power than seven sons of Sceva using the name of Jesus. It is hard to imagine that demons recognized Paul's handkerchief, and left people's bodies, but refused to depart when a priest's seven sons tried to cast them out using the name of Jesus. (Maybe there are such things as apostolic hankies . . .) But that is what happened. The demon's words were quite startling: "I recognize Jesus, and we know about Paul, but who are you?" When we come into submission to God's apostolic leaders, we are known in heaven and feared in hell. True heavenly authority causes angels to help us, and demons to respect our influence.

It's amazing that an apostle's hankie had more power than seven sons of Sceva using the name of Jesus.

Even the Gentile centurion in the book of Luke recognized that Jesus had authority to heal his sick servant, because he was a man under authority.

When we come into submission to God's apostolic leaders, we are known in heaven and feared in hell.

Now Jesus started on His way with them; and when He was not far from the house, the centurion sent friends, saying to Him, "Lord, do not trouble Yourself further, for I am not worthy for You to come under my roof; for this reason I did not even consider myself worthy to come to You, but just say the word, and my servant will be healed. For I also am a man placed under authority, with soldiers under me; and I say to this one, 'Go!' and he goes, and to another, 'Come!' and he comes, and to my slave, 'Do this!' and he does it." Now when Jesus heard this, He marveled at him, and turned and said to the crowd that was following Him, "I say to you, not even in Israel have I found such great faith" (Luke 7:6-9).

This is how true spiritual authority functions. We come in *sub*mission to the Father's mission and we get *co*mmissioned. Legitimate, anointed leaders carry an apostolic mission and are responsible to commission the Body of Christ. Even Jesus Himself said, "For I have come down from heaven, not to do My own will, but the will of Him who sent Me" (John 6:38). "I can do nothing on My own initiative. As I hear, I judge; and My judgment is just, because I do not seek My own will, but the will of Him who sent Me" (John 5:30). Was Jesus actually saying, "I really didn't want to do this miracle and redemption stuff. This is all my Father's idea"? No! He was simply demonstrating how apostles ("sent ones") receive authority. They yield their will to God and allow His plan to be carried out through their lives and the lives of those over whom they have authority. Like the 12 disciples Jesus sent out to spread the Kingdom, we also need to be sent and not just to go.

As we've seen, God has also commissioned angels to partner with His leaders in fulfilling their apostolic mission. When we are under God's authority, which includes being under His appointed leaders, we also partner with the angelic hosts. In Hebrews 1:14, it says of the angels, "Are they not all ministering spirits, sent out to render service for the sake of those who will inherit salvation?" The responsibility of the angels is to make sure that the sons and daughters of the King come into their divine destinies and fulfill the mission of the Kingdom.

Commissioning Angels

As I alluded to earlier, one of the most common ways the angels are commissioned is through prayer and prophecy. Consider the words of the psalmist:

Bless the LORD, you His angels, mighty in strength who *perform His word, obeying the voice of His word.* Bless you, the Lord, all His hosts, you who serve Him, doing His will.... Bless the LORD, all you works of His, in all places of His dominion; bless the LORD, oh my soul! (Psalm 103:20,22, emphasis added).

The angels heed the voice of His Word. The Church is His voice that declares His Word on earth. I don't think this means that we have to tell the angels what to do; I am simply saying that when we pray and prophesy in the name of the Lord, they hear the Word of the Lord and they go out and perform it. But we can only declare a Word of the Lord that commissions and sends the angels if we are under authority and therefore have authority.

Spiritual Covering

We find another indication of the nature and power of spiritual authority in a statement made by Stephen. Before he was stoned, he stood before his accusers and recounted a *Reader's Digest* version of the Old Testament, including the history of how Israel came to be enslaved in Egypt:

THERE AROSE ANOTHER KING OVER EGYPT WHO KNEW NOTHING ABOUT JOSEPH. It was he who took shrewd advantage of our race and mistreated our fathers so that they would expose their infants and they would not survive (Acts 7:18-19).

It is important to note that Stephen did not say there arose a king who knew not *God* and destroyed their race. Rather, he said, "There arose another king over Egypt who knew nothing about Joseph." Joseph's personal victories brought him to a position of favor and authority that released a corporate covering over his family. You know the story—Joseph's extended family, who believed he was dead, came to Egypt for food. When his brothers, the ones who had sold him into slavery, found out he was alive, they begged for their lives. He told them that what they meant for evil, God used for good. He forgave them and invited them to move to Egypt so they would be safe from the famine. Seventy members of his family relocated to Egypt, where Pharaoh gave them the best land. They multiplied and spread all over the nation, growing prosperous and remaining free. The Israelites lived a life of incredible blessing during the years of Joseph's rule, not because they deserved it, but because Joseph did (see Genesis 37–48)!

Why did Joseph deserve this blessing? What qualified him to carry such authority and favor? It wasn't his intelligence, education, charisma, people skills or any other quality by which human beings generally judge a person's leadership ability. Joseph rose to prominence for three reasons: (1) he lived supernaturally, demonstrated through his ability to interpret dreams; (2) in a dream he was called by God Himself to be a leader; (3) and he passed every test of his character on the way to his calling. Divine callings, proven character and a supernatural lifestyle are the three primary marks of a person with true spiritual authority.

Covering and Accountability

There is a difference between covering and accountability. Real accountability is only present in our lives when we have a personal relationship with people who can and do speak into our hearts, our circumstances and our relationships. Everyone needs these deep covenant connections—not primarily because they keep us from failing, but because they inspire us to reach for the high call of God that rests on each one of our lives. Historically, accountability has majored on helping people restrain their bad behavior. But as new creatures in Christ, we all need to be accountable to people who are regularly reminding each of us that we were born to make history! (That's why it's called account-ability and not account-disability.)

It is very unlikely that leaders who actually carry the apostolic mantles that provide the covering for entire movements will be able to provide relational accountability for most people under their covering. The very nature of their corporate responsibility prevents them from having the necessary time it takes to cultivate deep relationships with that many people, which is paramount for real discipleship and/or accountability. When it comes to those who operate in these roles, the truth of Proverbs applies: "A man of too many friends comes to ruin" (Proverbs 18:24).

The Lord Is My Shepherd

For many people reading this first chapter, the idea that someone has authority over us in God feels painful at best and impossible at worst. I know those feelings so well, having grown up with two stepfathers who abused their authority in my life. But the benefits of having true spiritual leadership in our lives far outweigh the internal struggle it takes to get there.

Some people who seem to have the greatest resistance to the concept of spiritual authority wouldn't dare tell their unsaved employer, "You can't tell me what to do. The Lord is my Shepherd. I don't submit to earthly authority." Instead, they go to work at the time their boss tells them to get there. They wear whatever the uniform or corporate code demands. They carry out the tasks that are required of them five or six days a week.

But on Sunday, they come to church and won't work in the nursery or perform some simple job that is asked of them. I have had believers tell me that the Shepherding Movement of the 1970s or some church leader hurt them and therefore they will never submit to spiritual authority ever again. Their life message is clear: "You can't tell me what to do." Can you imagine what your income would be like if you extended that way of thinking to the marketplace? It troubles me when Christians will do for money what they won't do for love!

It troubles me when Christians will do for money what they won't do for love!

Of course, there is always "spiritual leadership" in the Body of Christ who think it is their responsibility to control people instead of empower them to fulfill their God-given mandate. They use fear and manipulation to get their flock to do what they need done. These kinds of people should not be leaders and shouldn't be trusted or submitted to. True apostles always include the fulfillment of their people's dreams as part of their primary mission from God. Whenever shepherds lead in a way that doesn't significantly benefit their people, they are misusing their authority.

In fact, the first group of people a leader is called to minister to is his own family. The Scripture is clear that the foundation of a leader's authority is in managing his family relationships (see 1 Timothy 3:1-5). Many leaders have forgotten Paul's exhortation and have sacrificed their families on the altar of public ministry. It is imperative that fathers and mothers teach their sons and daughters to sacrifice. Sacrifice is a part of life in the Kingdom. But there is a huge difference between making a sacrifice and being sacrificed to obtain some "God-given purpose." If I could get a million people saved in Africa but it cost me one of my children, I would choose to keep my child. If I had to throw one of my kids under the bus to obtain some ministry goal, no matter how lofty the vision, my ministry would be built on a rotten foundation. I grieve for the children of many leaders and wonder what the heck those people are thinking by neglecting and mishandling their primary responsibilities.

Let me be clear: this is not the kind of leader that I am suggesting you trust. There is no such thing as a perfect leader, except Jesus. We can't require perfection from any leader. But we can expect those who lead us to demonstrate maturity, to love us and to live humbly.

The Move to Apostolic Families

As the Church makes this dramatic transition out of denominationalism and into apostolic families, it is paramount that we clearly understand the apostles' mantle and mandate so that governmental foundations can be laid that empower, rather than restrain, their extraordinary calling. In the next chapter, we will contrast the nature of traditional pastoral government with that of an apostolic structure in order to gain more insight into this new season.

Note
1. See Bethel Church's statement of faith at http://www.ibethel.org/we-believe.

2

The Emerging Apostolic Age

In times of change, learners inherit the Earth,
while the learned find themselves beautifully equipped to
deal with a world that no longer exists.

ERIC HOFFER

Old Manna

It was early Sunday morning, and the Bethel Church leadership team gathered as we do every week to pray for God to move miraculously among us. The atmosphere was charged as the small room filled up with about 30 passionate staff members, all eager for their chance to lead out in prayer. Each leader stood with anticipation, like racehorses waiting for the gate to open. My turn was near, so I formed my thoughts as the person next to me concluded his fervent exhortation. I was just about to blurt out, "I release the pool of Bethesda over Bethel Church," when the Lord suddenly interrupted my thinking.

"That's an old prophetic word!" He said.

I was stunned. I quickly reminded the Lord that just six months earlier He had told me that the church was like the pool of Bethesda.

"Lord, how could this be an old word?" I questioned.

"That's an old word!" the Lord repeated.

"What's the new word?" I asked, a bit sheepishly.

"My church is moving from the pool of Bethesda to Ezekiel's river," He said.

I had no idea what the Lord meant by that, but I quickly gathered my thoughts while the team waited and then boldly pronounced, "Bethel Church will be like Ezekiel's river!"

I still wasn't sure what Ezekiel's river had to do with the church, but as I prayed, I was getting rocked inside. I was eager to hang out with the Lord so that I could wrap my brain around the concept and get some understanding of what He and I were boldly declaring.

The Pool of Bethesda

As I sought the Lord, I began to realize that the kingdom of God is experiencing one of the greatest transitions in human history. The Lord showed me that the pool of Bethesda represents, in parable or picture form, where we are as the Church today; and the river in the book of Ezekiel characterizes where we are going. Let's begin by looking at the pool first in order to see the significance of this transition:

> Now there is in Jerusalem by the sheep gate a pool, which is called in Hebrew Bethesda, having five porticoes. In these lay a multitude of those who were sick, blind, lame, and withered, waiting for the moving of the waters; for an angel of the Lord went down at certain seasons into the pool and stirred up the water; whoever then first, after the stirring up of the water, stepped in was made well from whatever disease with which he was afflicted (John 5:2-4).

Did you notice that the pool of Bethesda had five porticoes? These kinds of details never used to mean much to me until I realized awhile ago the implication in what the apostle John said: "There are also many other things which Jesus did, which if they were written in detail, I suppose that even the world itself would not contain the books that would be written" (John 21:25). Because God reduced the things that were written about Jesus down to just a few hundred pages, then it stands to reason that every word He decided to include in His manuscript must be meaningful.

The details are also important because most of the Gospels are eyewitness accounts. If a person witnessed an accident between two automobiles, and happened to mention that both cars had hubcaps in recounting the story to a police officer, you would suspect that the hubcaps played some role in the accident. Otherwise, why would the person mention something so minor?

When the Lord first gave me the word about the Church being the pool of Bethesda, I was drawn to this description of the five porticoes surrounding the pool and began to consider their prophetic significance. The account in Scripture indicates that these porches were places of rest and covering for those needing healing, and provided access to the waters when the angel stirred them to release miracles. The Lord revealed to me that this was an awesome picture of the fivefold ministry (the apostle, prophet, evangelist, pastor and teacher). According to Ephesians 4:7-11, the fivefold ministers of Christ have each been commissioned to equip the saints for ministry. The five porticoes at the pool of Bethesda create an amazing picture of how these ministers, working together in unity, cover the Body of Christ, providing access to the raw power of God and the grace distributed by angels.

I came to understand that the fivefold ministry was transitioning by emerging out of obscurity and merging into the pool of unity. In other words, when the apostle, prophet, evangelist, pastor and teacher flow together and create a healthy governmental covering over the saints, this covering forms a kind of celestial vortex, creating strategic alliances with our heavenly allies. The implication of the word was that the Lord was establishing the fivefold ministry in His Church, and that the outcome would be increased angelic activity manifested by extraordinary miracles rarely witnessed in the history of the planet.

Two Governments

When I discovered the significance of the prophetic word about the pool, it was no wonder that the Lord's interruption in our prayer meeting that morning caught me off guard. Why would we need to be moving from this reality of unity, grace and power to something else? As I began to search out this new word and compare the picture of the pool of Bethesda with the metaphor of the river in the book of Ezekiel, a new aspect and a deeper revelation of the pool began to unfold.

The essence of this revelation is that, while the pool of Bethesda, with its five porticoes, does speak of the five ministry roles in Ephesians, it also represents a governmental structure that is fundamentally different from the organization represented by Ezekiel's river. The pool represents a *pastorate* and the river an *apostleship*.

By now you are probably wondering what the heck I am talking about. In order to explain these types of government, first let me back up a little bit and explain what I mean by "government." First of all, we need to understand that there is a difference between *government* and *governors*. I confused these terms for years. I used to preach that the five-fold ministry was the "government of God." Then one day I had a revelation that *government* was actually the *structure* in which *governors*, who are the *officials*, govern. I also came to understand that *leadership* was the *art of governing*. Through this revelation I realized how important government is to governors. A governmental structure either empowers or constrains the ability of governors to lead effectively.

I had a revelation that *government* was actually the *structure* in which *governors*, who are the *officials*, govern.

Government by the People, for the People

We can see the difference between government and governors by looking at our own American government. When our forefathers drafted our Constitution, they were interested in creating a very different governmental structure than the British monarchy that once ruled them. They thought Britain's king had way too much power. In response, they created a constitutional republic fashioned to limit our president's authority, and balance the decision-making power among the branches of government and the majority of citizens.

As our forefathers contemplated our young country's future, they realized that if our nation were ever to be under siege by an enemy on our own shores, a government with all these checks and balances would process decisions too slowly to win a war. With this in mind, they provided something in our Constitution called *martial law*. When Congress enacts martial law, our governmental structure is transformed from a constitutional republic to a military government, which empowers the role of the president above the other two branches of government. Martial law means our commander-in-chief can lead our troops without having to get the battle plan approved by the majority, thereby giving him or her the ability to make quick decisions, which are necessary to win a war. Unless martial law is enacted, the United States could have the greatest military general in history as its president, but the *governmental structure* itself would restrict his or her ability to lead our forces into victory in the event of a siege inside our borders. This is a great example of how a governmental structure can either empower or restrain its governors.

Designing Governmental Structures

For a long time I have watched organizations build governmental structures around leaders that hamstring those leaders' God-given abilities, and then later blame them for not performing well. It is crucial that we understand the three main factors that great governments must consider if they are going to be successful. These factors are: *Who is leading? Who are the people they are leading? And, in what epoch season are they leading these people?* (Biblically speaking, an "epoch season" is a *way* in which God deals with a certain people in a certain time.) Misunderstanding any of these factors will cause governmental structures to be formed that limit, resist or even derail their people's God-given purposes.

Organizations could learn a great lesson from the contractor who built our community college in Redding, California. When Shasta College was constructed several years ago, the contractor didn't install the sidewalks immediately after finishing the buildings. Instead, he planted lawns around the entire campus and took a year to observe where people wore out the grass. Then the contractor poured sidewalks in the worn sections of the lawn so that the walkways best facilitated the destination of the students and faculty.

Government should be like those sidewalks. Governmental structures are the paths that are supposed to facilitate the gifts, passions and purposes of the God-given destinies of both the people who are leading and those being led, as well as the epoch season in which they are leading. But often organizations construct sidewalks (government) with little or no regard for these factors. In so doing they make it hard, if not impossible, for the people operating in these organizations to embrace their dreams and fulfill their destinies.

On the other hand, great organizations are developed when their leaders carefully analyze these three dynamics and then build governmental structures that best empower them. The outcome of this kind of formation is that it actually facilitates the organization's destiny instead of constraining it.

The Pool Versus the River

With this in mind, let's look at the contrast between the pool of Bethesda and Ezekiel's river and see how the governmental structures they represent, the *pastorate* and the *apostleship,* relate to the three factors of government listed above.

The pastorate defines the three factors of government as follows: The leader is a pastor, which is essentially a shepherd. Like a shepherd gathering his sheep, the pastor has a God-given anointing to gather people and tend to their needs. The people who follow the shepherd are obviously sheep—people whose primary job is to stay together and stay healthy. Pastorates thrive when people perceive the season to be one in which these goals of staying together and staying healthy define their primary purpose.

The typical pastorate structure is seen clearly in the picture of the pool of Bethesda, where people *gathered* in order to have a supernatural encounter. They had to be there in the right season and they had to be the first person in the pool when the angel stirred the water to have a supernatural encounter.

People come to most churches today for the same reason. If you want to be touched by God, you come to church. If you need to get saved, you come to church. If you need to be healed, counseled, taught or delivered, you need to come to church. You get the idea. The emphasis is on coming to church, and thus the meetings are designed to meet the various needs of the Body. It also seems to me that what was true of the pool of Bethesda is generally true of pastorates—miracles happen in pastorates, but they are infrequent and inconsistent. There are seasonal visitations, but many still lie along the edge of the pool awaiting their turn for an encounter.

Ezekiel's river provides us with a very different picture:

Then he brought me back to the door of the house; and behold, water was flowing from under the threshold of the house toward the east, for the house faced east. And the water was flowing down from under, from the right side of the house, from south of the altar. He brought me out by way of the north gate and led me around on the outside to the outer gate by way of the gate that faces east. And behold, water was trickling from the south side. When the man went out toward the east with a line in his hand, he measured a thousand cubits, and he led me through the water, water reaching the ankles. Again he measured a thousand and led me through the water, water reaching the knees. Again he measured a thousand and led me through the water, water reaching the loins. Again he measured a thousand; and it was a river that I could not ford, for the water had risen, enough water to swim in, and a river that could not be forded. He said to me, "Son of man, have you seen this?" Then he brought me back to the bank of the river. Now when I had returned, behold, on the bank of the river there were very many trees on the one side and on the other. Then he said to me, "These waters go out toward the eastern region and go down into the Arabah; then they go toward the sea, being made to flow into the sea, and the waters of the sea become fresh. It will come about that every living creature which swarms in every place where the river goes, will live. And there will be very many fish, for these waters go there and the others become fresh; so everything will live where the river goes. And it will come about that fishermen will stand beside it; from Engedi to Eneglaim there will be a place for the spreading of nets. Their fish will be according to their kinds, like the fish of the Great Sea, very many. But its swamps and marshes will not become fresh; they will be left for salt. By the river on its bank, on one side and on the other, will grow all kinds of trees for food. Their leaves will not wither and their fruit will not fail. They will bear every month because their water flows from the sanctuary, and their fruit will be for food and their leaves for healing (Ezekiel 47:1-12).

There's a lot of revelation we can gather from this vision. First of all, notice that this river, which, like the water in the pool, represents the grace of God, flows out from under the sanctuary door and becomes deeper the further it gets from the sanctuary.

This depicts a *movement* in which God's presence grows more powerful as the *people of God* take His presence into the world—businesses, homes, schools, and so forth—with them. The further the saints get from the sanctuary, the deeper the grace of God penetrates the darkness. In other words, the greatest miracles, the most powerful expressions of the Kingdom, are destined to happen in the worst places on the planet, not inside the walls of a building.

In the pastorate model, the needy come to a central location to get healed—the pool—but in the apostolic governmental model, the river flows through our cities and everyone it touches gets healed and becomes fresh. This river metaphor fits an apostleship so well because the word "apostle" means "sent one." Pastors *gather*, like the pool, but apostles *send*, like the river.

Apostles are not only *sent*; they are sent for a very specific purpose. The word "apostle" comes from the secular Roman world. The Romans were very aggressive about expanding their empire. They wisely employed the strategy of Alexander the Great, who established the Greek Empire by conquering kingdoms and then culturizing them in the Greek ways. Without establishing culture, these conquered peoples would not assimilate into their new national identity and government. The Romans developed envoys to culturize their conquered cities in Roman ways, so that when the people were in Rome, they would do as the Romans. Roman generals called *apostles* most often led these envoys.

It is interesting that when Jesus promoted His disciples from learners to leaders, He didn't call them "patriarchs." They would have had some idea of how patriarchs led, as there was an Old Testament model already in place for them. Neither did He call them priests, prophets or rabbis, because again there were patterns of order already developed for those roles. Instead He called them by a Roman title that would forever define their ministry responsibility and authority. Like the Roman armies who first battled for territory and then educated the conquered people in the Roman ways, the apostles of Jesus were commissioned to displace the powers of darkness with the power of God and replace the enemy's authority with the government of God, bringing the ways of the Kingdom to influence every aspect of society.

We see the mission of apostles expressed in the only "model" prayer Jesus taught His leaders to pray. Jesus said, "Pray, then, in this way: 'Our Father who is in heaven, hallowed be Your name. Your kingdom come. Your will be done, on earth as it is in heaven'" (Matthew 6:9-10). The emphasis in the Lord's Prayer is that earth would become like heaven. In the same way the Romans were to make their conquered cities look like Rome, we have been commissioned to pull heaven down to earth until the will of God is done here exactly as it is there!

The emphasis in the Lord's Prayer is that earth would become like heaven.

This commission defines the nature of an apostolic structure of government. An apostleship defines the three factors of government as follows: The leader is an apostle, one sent to establish the culture of heaven on earth. Those who follow an apostle are those who seek to have heaven manifest in their lives, and to be sent out to release heaven wherever they go. Apostleships thrive in a season when people perceive that their primary purpose is to transform the culture of earth with the culture of heaven.

Making the Transition

In late 2007, the Lord spoke to me and said, "Mankind has just entered into the new apostolic age. Yet the modern world has never experienced the true power of an apostle, because apostles have emerged in a pastorate form of government that restricts, constrains and often usurps their ability to govern." For the most part, the Church has only empowered her apostles to plant churches. But apostles were never meant merely to be church planters: they were called to be world changers!

A leader can plant 100 churches in different cities around the world, but if those churches don't bring cultural transformation to their cities, then they are not apostolic. Cultural transformation is synonymous with apostolic ministry. Think about it. If we gather 5,000 people week after week on Sunday mornings in a city of half a million, and yet the crime rate remains unchanged, the cancer rate is unaffected, the divorce rate continues to grow and the economy is in decline, what does that say about the people of God in that city? If we are supposed to be salt and light, and all the nations of the earth are to be blessed in us, then isn't it true that the negative statistics of our cities are a commentary on us? Look at the commentary on the first-century church: The rulers of the city were crying out, "These who have turned the world upside down have come here too" (Acts 17:6, *NKJV*). What does it say about us if we can't even change one city with thousands of believers?

The truth is, a pastorate form of government is not designed to transform cities. It is developed to attract people, to create a culture where flocks gather to get healthy and happy. Pastorates are, to some degree, irrelevant to their city's culture because their governmental structures are built to congregate, not to deploy. This principle is evident when you look at American cities statistically. Demographically, the U.S. cities that have the greatest Christian, churchgoing population density also have some of the worst social statistics in our country (with the exception of a few cities). In other words, the cities that have the highest crime rates, the most divorces, the greatest amount of abortions per capita, the highest levels of poverty and the poorest health statistics also have the best church attendance. What we need to understand is that gathering believers for two hours on Sunday morning is *not* synonymous with cultural transformation! Pastorates are simply culturally ineffective by design.

Apostleships, on the other hand, are developed around the principle of training, equipping and deploying the saints to radically alter society. The primary message of apostleships is that the kingdom of God is at hand, and their main strategy is to demonstrate the raw power of God in the darkest places on the planet. The apostolic government, like Ezekiel's river, creates a supernatural atmosphere that affects everything it touches, from the fish (people) in the river to the trees (nations and cities) along its banks. Wherever the river flows, things get healed, become fresh and are supernaturally productive (producing fruit every month instead of one season a year). This river is the perfect metaphor for the emerging apostolic age.

The primary message of apostleships is that the kingdom of God is at hand.

Apostleships Empower Pastorates

Obviously, in order to deploy people into the darkest places of the planet, the saints need to be gathered, healthy and happy. It is impossible for us to create a culture around us that we don't have within us. Therefore, it is essential for apostleships to build and empower pastorates within them that develop happy and healthy sheep. In fact, depending on the apostle's *metron* (Greek for "measure"), an apostleship may have many pastorates under its covering. The transition from a pastorate to an apostolic form of government does not eliminate the pastorate, but repositions it within the greater purpose of the apostolic mission.

This epoch season change is one in which God is still emphasizing *gathering*, but in the context of *deployment*. Pastorates will still gather the sheep, but they won't seek to get them healthy and happy simply as ends in themselves, but as preparation for being sent out to change the world.

Working in Harmony

It is paramount that the fivefold governors merge in a way that facilitates their proper places in Christ and empowers them to operate in their God-given roles. This will result in the Body being equipped with the grace to build *itself* up in love as it accomplishes the Great Commission to make disciples of all nations. As the Church makes this transition, meetings like Sunday morning services will be transformed from social gatherings into Holy Spirit supernatural training sessions! Our services will continue to embrace worship, fellowship, healing, prophecy, teaching, and so on, but with the apostolic purpose of cultural reformation at their core.

In the book of Isaiah there is a great example of the fruit of pastoral ministry and apostolic mission flowing together. First, Isaiah the prophet pronounces the restoration of individual people in every dimension of their lives:

> The Spirit of the Lord GOD is upon me, because the LORD has anointed me to bring good news to the afflicted; He has sent me to bind up the brokenhearted,

to proclaim liberty to captives and freedom to prisoners; to proclaim the favorable year of the LORD and the day of vengeance of our God; to comfort all who mourn, to grant those who mourn in Zion, giving them a garland instead of ashes, the oil of gladness instead of mourning, the mantle of praise instead of a spirit of fainting. So they will be called oaks of righteousness, the planting of the LORD, that He may be glorified (Isaiah 61:1-3).

Then Isaiah goes on to prophesy that these same people who experienced personal transformation are to be commissioned to rebuild their cities:

Then they will rebuild the ancient ruins, they will raise up the former devastations; and they will repair the ruined cities, the desolations of many generations (Isaiah 61:4).

This is a great example of the teamwork that is to take place between apostles and pastors, resulting in happy and healthy people having a dynamic, positive impact on their cities. We need the entire fivefold ministry working in harmony together like a beautiful orchestra, the apostle being the conductor.

The Bethel Story

When Bill and Beni Johnson became the senior leaders of Bethel Church in 1996, the church was definitely a pastorate. They replaced Ray Larson, a true fivefold pastor with a real passion for the lost. It was a lampstand church, and under his leadership, the fellowship had become a great place for people to get saved and discipled. He and his leadership team did a great job of growing the church from a few hundred people to a congregation of nearly

2,000 over a period of eight years. They developed leaders for church ministry, emphasized connections in social gatherings, formed sports teams, produced large Christmas and Easter performances and community events, established Christian schools, and the like. People felt connected and taken care of.

Kathy and I joined Bill in 1998. The church was already in the midst of a very quick transition from a pastorate to an apostleship. Bill is an amazing apostle with a mandate to reform the Church, and I am a prophet with a passion for cultural transformation. Under this new mission, Bethel became a catalyst for a movement focused on the core values of the goodness of God and the supernatural power of the Spirit.

But what became evident behind the scenes was that we had a desperate need for a pastorate within our movement. It's not that we didn't have pastors on staff. We did. We actually had eight pastors on our team. What we lacked was the structure that facilitated their strength, valued their ministry approach and empowered their need for a greater relational context in our church.

What we discovered in this season at Bethel Church is that pastors need a pastorate form of government to be successful, but that most of them cannot build the structure themselves. It takes a special pastor/builder to pour the necessary sidewalks, so to speak, that ensure reaching the destiny of their office and calling.

Another important component necessary to empower pastors successfully is that apostles and prophets need to be sensitive to the pastoral perspective and worldview. The very virtue of the pastoral calling causes them to have a dramatically different approach to life. In some ways, apostolic and prophetic core values can sometimes seem to undermine those that reinforce pastoral care. For example, apostles and prophets, by nature, tend to emphasize miracles, healings and other supernatural interventions of God. The instant, immediate and spontaneous tend to be highlighted in apostleships. The side effect of this perspective is that the prolonged pastoral processes of restoration common in the counseling, discipleship and caring for those chronically ill who have yet to experience healing can seem to be devalued. True fivefold pastors work best in a highly relational environment where they can love people into wholeness over time.

Bill and I began to realize that we needed someone who could build highways that empowered our pastoral ministry. With this in mind, in 2001, we brought Danny and Sheri Silk to our team to develop a pastorate structure. Over the next five years, they assembled and empowered a pastoral team that nurtured our people into health. Danny started our Transformation Center, which incorporates more than 50 anointed people he trained in the counseling and deliverance ministry. Next, he built the Pastor On Call ministry for people with emergencies who can't wait for an appointment. Under Danny's guidance, volunteers staff most of this ministry. He empowered a team that ministers to those waiting for healing. Recently, he developed the School of Transformation, which trains and equips leaders in our apostolic network to reproduce healthy cultures in their own local churches. Danny and Sheri are a great example of gifted pastors who can replicate themselves and know how to build pastorate governmental structures.

The Structure and the Right Ingredients

All of the fivefold ministers need governmental structures that empower their strengths and cover their weaknesses. We have only concentrated on two of them in this chapter. But without government that is specifically developed for prophets, teachers and evangelists, they will be largely ineffective also.

One of the symptoms of governmental dysfunction is the overemphasis or underemphasis of a particular office. For example, if the pastoral ministry has "freeways" to run on, and the prophetic ministry has "rugged trails" to traverse, safety will be overemphasized and adventure and risk will be underemphasized. Pastors work to create safe places for people to grow up in. They love predictable environments that don't scare the flock. But this can lead them to downplay other elements of Christ's nature. We need to remember that the same Jesus who made sinners feel at home with Him also overturned tables, drove money changers out of the Temple with a whip, called a woman a dog and ostracized the religious leaders of His day.

If there is insufficient evangelistic grace flowing into the congregational pool, the Church will stagnate with old growth, and succession planning will be virtually nonexistent. If the evangelistic ministry is overstated (which is impossible, according to most evangelists), the Church, metaphorically speaking, will be a huge nursery with nobody qualified to care for infants.

When the Body lacks the adequate influence of true fivefold teachers, biblical foundations give way to subjective experiences and feelings. When the teacher's role is overemphasized, Christians will typically be overinformed and underexperienced.

It takes all the fivefold offices—apostles, prophets, evangelists, pastors and teachers—to equip a fully functioning Body. Every baker knows that it doesn't just take the right ingredients to make a great cookie; it takes the right amount of each ingredient. Good government empowers the entire fivefold ministry proportionally so there is the right amount of each ingredient (office) in the Body of Christ.

3

"Mr. Gorbachev, Tear Down This Wall!"

Great spirits have always found violent opposition from mediocrities. The latter cannot understand it when a man does not thoughtlessly submit to hereditary prejudices but honestly and courageously uses his intelligence.

ALBERT EINSTEIN

Serpents and Doves

If we really are in a new epoch season where God is leading us out of the stale bread of denominationalism into the fresh manna of apostleships, and the main manifestation of apostleships is cultural transformation, then we must ask ourselves: How do we practically bring the Kingdom's influence to bear on this ailing planet? Is there a way to expose 6 billion people to our amazing King and make a way for His superior Kingdom to revolutionize the world's mindsets?

Jesus said, "Behold, I send you out as sheep in the midst of wolves; so be shrewd as serpents and innocent as doves" (Matthew 10:16). He also said, "The sons of this age are more shrewd in relation to their own kind than the sons of light"

(Luke 16:8). It is time for us to study the tactics of serpents and the sons of this age so that we can emulate their strategies and overcome their purposes!

It is time for us to study the tactics of serpents and the sons of this age so that we can emulate their strategies and overcome their purposes!

An Empire Crumbles

Let me give you a few examples of worldly tactics that have greatly influenced the course of history and contrast them with the Church's approach to see if we can gain some valuable insights.

I started the first grade in 1961, at the height of the Cold War. I have vivid memories of our elementary school teachers instructing us on how to respond in the case of a Russian attack. Eight hundred kids, their little hearts pounding out of their chests, would practice scrambling for "safety" under their small desks as the air raid alarm screamed over the PA system.

I still remember lying awake at night as a young boy, envisioning warplanes flying over our house and dropping bombs on our neighborhood. I would pull the covers over my head, trembling at the thoughts that were pressed into my young mind. My uncle Joe, who lived a couple of miles away from us, spent two years and thousands of dollars turning his backyard into an underground bomb shelter. I can still recall my parents having conversations with us about meeting them in my uncle's bomb shelter in the case of an air raid. Radio stations would practice their emergency broadcasting system alerts about once a month.

Of course they would tell you before and after the alert, "This is just a test of the emergency broadcasting system." Boy, if you happened to turn the radio on in the middle of one of those "tests," you had to wait for what seemed like an eternity to find out if your neighborhood was under attack!

Those were times of uncertainty, high anxiety and extreme apprehension. But something happened between those early years of grade school and 1989. Without a shot fired or a bomb dropped, the Iron Curtain disintegrated. It really had little to do with the threat of the American military. Instead, this was an inside job. President Reagan had called on Russian president Mikhail Gorbachev to tear down the literal wall that separated East Germany and West Germany and the greater "wall" between communist nations and the rest of the world. That's exactly what happened.

The people in those nations tore down the wall of communism all by themselves. But after years of fear, threats and intimidation, how did communism suddenly fall like a house of cards? Well, that's a great question that has long been debated by some of the brightest minds of our time. Certainly Ronald Reagan, Margaret Thatcher, Pope John Paul II, Lech Walesa, Mikhail Gorbachev and Boris Yeltsin had much to do with it! But the simple answer is that a major transition took place *inside* of the hearts of the Communist people, which demanded that they be treated differently from the outside.

Meet the Beatles

When the Beatles made their début in the mid-1960s, the Russian KGB heard their music and outlawed their albums. The only way to purchase a Beatles album in the USSR in those days was on the black market where they were sold for more than a hundred dollars each! Why were they outlawed, you might ask? Because the Russians believed that if their citizens were exposed to the Beatles' music, they would realize there were happy people in the world and overthrow their oppressive government.

It turns out that these fears were not entirely unfounded. In one of the documentaries I watched on the USSR, the commentator actually attributed the end of the Cold War and the fall of communism to the Beatles.[1] This is a gross exaggeration of the facts, but there is a measure of truth in his point. People are transformed from the inside when they are exposed to new ideas from the outside. Whether these ideas are true or false, internal change takes place as long as the people who are exposed to them embrace the information as accurate. (Of course, transformation in itself isn't necessarily positive. The long-term effects of these ideas are primarily determined by whether or not the concepts are actually true.)

In one of the documentaries on the USSR, the commentator actually attributed the end of the Cold War and the fall of communism to the Beatles.

It is interesting that we call new ideas *in-formation*. Thoughts really do form structures inside of people that eventually demand new structures around them. As internal metamorphosis begins to take place, people's external circumstances, which were once congruent with their lifestyle, become conscious barriers and restrictions to their new sense of purpose and destiny.

Ultimately, new mindsets perpetuate transitional epoch season changes, which most often result in forcing governmental shifts. Out of the rubble of such upheavals, new leadership paradigms begin to emerge.

Lesson from Iraq

Great leaders understand that real change can only take place when people are transformed from the inside out, not from the outside in. The invisible kingdom inside a person ultimately becomes the visible kingdom around them.

The invisible kingdom inside a person ultimately becomes the visible kingdom around them.

The war in Iraq taught us some profound lessons about this principle. We learned (and are still learning) the hard way that displacing an evil dictator isn't nearly as difficult as replacing him. We overthrew Saddam Hussein in 37 days and declared victory on the deck of the aircraft carrier *USS Abraham Lincoln*. But we have spent several more years and the lives of many more soldiers trying to establish a democracy in a region that has has been dominated by tyranny for hundreds of years.

The real challenge is how to alter people's worldview when it has been distorted by wrong core values. For example, the highest core value of democracy is freedom that transfers power to the people. The greatest challenge of replacing a dictatorship with a democracy is teaching people who have lived in virtual slavery how to make healthy choices for themselves and by themselves. Free citizens are given the right and the responsibility to make up their own minds, to decide who is going to lead them and to vote for the laws that will guide their society. But often people who are liberated after being controlled all their lives don't know how to behave in a culture of freedom, and they soon construct other prisons for themselves.

The mindset of the Iraqi people is compounded by the predominant national religion, Islam, which by its very nature creates a culture of control. It requires extreme discipline and submission to leadership. It has little value for freedom, liberty and independence.

On the other hand, like it or not, a democratic government has emerged in Iraq, which at its core comes from Greek beginnings and is heavily influenced by a Judeo-Christian worldview that values freewill over control. (Remember, it is the Christian Bible that teaches us that God put two trees in the Garden. From the beginning of creation, it was the God of the Bible, not the God of the Koran, that instituted the concept of freewill and choice. We will talk about this more later in this book.)

The outcome of Iraq still lies in the balance, but the greatest battle is not being fought in the streets of Baghdad or any other Iraqi city. The supreme conflict is being waged on the battlefield of the hearts and minds of men and women. The future of Iraq will ultimately be determined by the culture that is cultivated inside the souls of its people.

The future of Iraq will ultimately be determined by the culture that is cultivated inside the souls of its people.

War of Ideas

How is this inner battle fought? What are the weapons of this warfare, and how is victory ascertained? These are the questions great leaders must ask and understand if we are going to be effective in helping to create a global reformation.

People are transformed as they are exposed to new ideas and embrace them. The need for exposure is obvious; people cannot become what they haven't yet seen and/or heard. The Church understands this very well. We are convinced that preaching the Word of God to people transforms them. But what we often fail to understand is that people only embrace the ideas in which they find value, and they receive them best from people who have favor in their lives. The million-dollar question is: How do we get people to value Kingdom ideas when they don't?

> **People cannot become what they haven't yet seen and/or heard.**

Think about it: how did the Beatles propagate their radical new philosophies to the masses? They hid their message in music that everyone loved. People valued their melodies, which in turn caused folks to like the Beatles and eventually it led the masses to embrace their lyrics. These are the elements required for true transformation to transpire inside of people: They must be exposed to new ideas and they have to like the messenger as well as value the message.

> **We only have as much influence in people's lives as they have value for us.**

Christians have a hard time understanding that we only have as much influence in people's lives as they have value for us. Any time our influence in the lives of people transcends the level of value we have in their lives, our ideas will be rejected and the ability to bring true change is lost. Actually, people feel manipulated when we try to persuade them beyond the boundaries of the significance we have in their eyes.

Lesson from the Homosexual Community

The homosexual community in America has mastered this principle of connecting their agendas with something people value in order to change their mindset. For example, have you ever watched HGTV? It's supposed to be the home improvement channel. But there is a subtle yet *very powerful* message being proclaimed in their approach to home improvement. The message is that the homosexual lifestyle is normal. Although less than 3 percent of Americans are homosexual, a very high percentage of HGTV episodes feature homosexual couples.

Home improvement is a brilliant backdrop for propagating the homosexual agenda. First of all, it connects straight people who have a similar interest in home improvement with homosexuals. There is a hidden message being proclaimed in this connection that heterosexuals and homosexuals have "lots" in common. Second, it allows the producers to portray homosexual couples in a home setting, looking like traditional families. Many of these shows portray homosexual couples with their children as they are buying, improving or renovating their homes. Their point is clear: "Come in and have a look around. You will see how much we are like any other married couple. Our family is no different from your family." By attaching their message to something people value, those advocating the normalcy of homosexuality gain a platform to expose their audience to their radical ideas.

Their strategy is so well thought out that it astounds me. The majority of their shows also feature heterosexual people. You might ask, why would they show straight couples at all if their agenda is to promote the homosexual lifestyle? They show both because they know that if HGTV only featured homosexuals on their shows, their audience would be reduced to the small percentage of the population who are already gay or sympathetic to their cause. They would lose their ability to proclaim their message to the masses. You can bet that HGTV is not trying to entertain homosexuals; they are trying to convert heterosexuals to their viewpoint! It's gay and lesbian evangelism hidden in the disguise of home improvement. Let me tell you—it is a brilliant plan, and it is working.

In the last 20 years, homosexual agendas have leveraged massive control on the climate of our nation, and they are accomplishing this with just a small pool of the populace. In a 2002 Gallup poll, Americans were asked what percentage of the population they thought was homosexual. Their answers were revealing. The citizens polled thought the percentage of gay and lesbian residents in the U.S.A. was somewhere around 20 percent! Remember, it is less than 3 percent. (Even the National Gay and Lesbian Task Force estimates that homosexuals are 3 to 8 percent of the population.[2]) It is very hard for the average person to conceive that such a small percentage of the population could leverage so much control over a country.

Have you ever noticed that unlike HGTV, most of our religious TV programs are produced by Christians, for Christians? Usually somewhere in the program the producers will throw in some kind of evangelistic message so all the prebelievers who are *not* watching will embrace the Kingdom's cause and get born again.

When are we, as Christians, going to start being strategic about our influence? We are so darn unstrategic that it's embarrassing! We go to gay pride parades and hold up picket signs, protesting their lifestyle in the name of God. I guess we just want to make sure the homosexual community knows how we feel about their sexual orientation. Boy, those picket signs are having such huge impact on the gay and lesbian community. They are falling to their knees in the streets, begging God for forgiveness. *Not!*

Hated for the Cause of Christ

Sometimes I think we do things as believers just to soothe our conscience. We are not really stupid enough to believe that our protest signs, for instance, are actually influencing gays and lesbians. Picket signs certainly aren't what Jesus had in mind when He sent us out to do *signs* and wonders. But to a powerless church, signs have become something you nail to a stick! I think it just makes us feel like we are radical Christians when we take a stand for righteousness. It doesn't seem to occur to us that we are actually hurting our cause by destroying any value we have with the homosexual population. The age-old adage is still true: People don't care what you know until they know that you care.

To a powerless church, signs have become something you nail to a stick!

Offending the Masses

I was teaching at a ministry school awhile back, and as I entered the classroom, some of the students were in front of the class sharing testimonies from an outreach they had done at the downtown mall the day before. The first "testimony" was that the security guards had kicked them out of the mall for trying to minister to customers in the stores. As they recounted the story, the class erupted in shouting, clapping and cheering.

I sat there grieved. There is no glory in offending the people we are trying to reach, for no purpose, especially in a country where our right to free speech is protected. The goal is to love people into the Kingdom.

Certainly you may be rejected in the process of extending that love, and Jesus told us not to be surprised by that kind of persecution. He even said, "Blessed are you when men hate you, and ostracize you, and insult you, and scorn your name as evil, for the sake of the Son of Man" (Luke 6:22). But there is a big difference between being hated for the "sake of the Son of Man" and being rejected because we are under the influence of the spirit of stupid, rude or ridiculous.

Some people have a martyr's complex that has perverted their sense of justice. They are under the delusion that any time they share the gospel with someone and get the cold shoulder, somehow they got rejected for the cause of Christ. They take the verses about true persecution in the Bible to mean that being disliked by unbelievers is a good sign. But nowhere did Jesus tell us that rejection was the goal. We must not confuse the purpose with the process.

We must not confuse the purpose with the process.

My Story

I have often wanted to find a place to hide while watching certain Christians preach to people. I was so embarrassed by the way they were treating the very people they were trying to "minister" to. With their attitude, they could have been giving away thousand-dollar bills and they still would have been rejected. But I must be honest—my perception of that kind of ministry first developed through my own experience of learning that radical doesn't mean rude. We need methods that don't undermine our message.

In 1977, Kathy and I moved our family from the San Francisco Bay Area to a small community of 3,000 in the mountains of Northern California where we lived for the next 21 years. We owned several automotive businesses in those days, including a Union 76 service station located on Main Street. In front of the service station, right next to the street, we had a large double-sided reader board where we displayed different quotes or messages every day.

In the late eighties, Planned Parenthood, the leading abortion provider in the country, was determined to put a clinic in our community. The entire Christian community was very upset about this. I decided to lead a movement against Planned Parenthood to stop them from establishing a clinic in our town. I thoroughly researched their organization, examining their founder, their history and the impact they had on other cities. Then I put the message PLANNED PARENTHOOD GO HOME on one side of our reader board and ABORTION IS MURDER on the other side. I left that sign up for months.

I went to all of the Planned Parenthood community meetings, taking a couple hundred Christians with me each time. We completely overpowered the 20 or 30 pro-Planned Parenthood people who attended the meetings. As soon as the Planned Parenthood leaders started to speak, I would stand up, interrupt them and ask them pointed questions. Of course, they couldn't give an honest or direct answer to any of my questions without being lynched by the prolife crowd. So the crowd cheered and applauded at my every question. Their leaders were quite intimidated by the overall climate of the mob. Who could blame them?

Finally, the issue came to our board of supervisors to be decided. They had to cancel the first meeting and move it to a larger facility to handle the crowds, where again, we showed up in overwhelming force. When the supervisors invited the speakers from different perspectives to come to the microphone and share, I spoke for the prolifers as they cheered and applauded. When others shared a different point of view, we sneered, booed and let everyone in the room know that we had no respect for them or their opinions. But by the time the meeting was over, the board of supervisors had overwhelmingly voted to allow Planned Parenthood to set up a clinic in our community, where they remain to this day!

As you might imagine, I have thought a lot about this experience in an effort to understand it. I am still not exactly sure what happened there that day. I don't know if those on the board of supervisors were actually voting in favor of Planned Parenthood or if they were deciding against the disrespect we showed our opponents. Even more sobering to me has been the question of whether or not our attitude tied God's hands and kept Him from acting on our behalf. I am sure we represented His perspectives on the abortion issue accurately, but we sure didn't display His heart toward those who disagreed with us. We dishonored, devalued and disrespected people made in God's image so that we could make our point that those "prochoice" people had no value for the human life carried in the womb of a woman. To us, the end justified the means. We didn't care about the process because we were sure we had the purpose right.

Several years later, I went through a process of identifying and writing down the virtues by which I vowed to live the rest of my life. The fifth virtue on my list came from my experience with Planned Parenthood. It reads: "I will treat all people with respect, whether they are friend or foe, as they were created in God's image." This does not mean that I am opposed to peaceful protesting or other public displays of disapproval. But I am opposed to disrespecting, dishonoring and/or performing acts of hatred toward anyone, whether I agree with their values or not.

We Might as Well Join 'Em

On the other end of the spectrum, there is an entire segment of the religious community that is terrified of offending anyone. They've given up on overcoming sin and instead have become just like sinners. They have decided that if you can't beat 'em, then you might as well join 'em. Of course, they've had to alter the gospel just a little to embrace things like the homosexual lifestyle and abortion, for example. Not much; only slight changes to the Bible were necessary. Not! These folks try to stay socially relevant, not just by welcoming sinners into their congregations (which all churches should do), but also by *ordaining* them as leaders so that they won't upset anyone!

We need to learn how to disagree with someone's sin and still sincerely love and embrace the person.

This strategy is just as destructive as violating respect and honor in proclaiming the gospel to people. We need to learn how to disagree with someone's sin and still sincerely love and embrace the person. Jesus did this so well that sinners even invited Him to their drinking parties (see Luke 7:34; 15:1-2). But He never compromised His standards or took on their lifestyle to be accepted by them. His love for them simply transcended their fear of Him. What a great lesson for all of us!

Denominationalism

I wrote earlier about how denominationalism has affected the way in which Christians relate to one another, gathering when they agree and dividing when they disagree. But probably the greatest impact denominationalism has had on our planet is not the way believers treat one another but the way they relate to the world.

Because denominationalism views disagreement as an enemy, the goal of all relational interaction is to convince people, "We are right." For example, if I have a friendship with a homosexual person, it has to be for the sole purpose of converting that person to "Christianity." The religious community will not give me permission to have a relationship with someone I don't agree with unless I have an agenda. This leads to what I call the "car lot syndrome." When we step onto a car lot and the salesperson approaches us, we all know the drill. "Good afternoon, sir. Lovely day, isn't it? Boy, that is a beautiful pair of jeans you have on. I don't believe I have ever seen a pair of jeans like that before." And the beat goes on. Everyone knows the salesperson doesn't give a rip about our jeans, our hair or the fact that we don't sweat much for a heavy person. They are just trying to sell us a car.

When we approach non-Christians with a denominational mindset, we have an agenda. The non-Christian person knows that we are only in a relationship to sell Jesus to him (or her). Nothing we say or do feels sincere. But what would happen if we honestly just loved people without an agenda? What would life be like if we had an authentic interest in him or her as a person?

When we approach non-Christians with a denominational mindset, we have an agenda.

Is President Obama the Antichrist?

The other day I got a long email "proving" that President Obama was the Antichrist! I wrote the sender back and said, "At least the Antichrist is not the Pope this time." Receipt of such an email is a manifestation of the denominational spirit at its worst. In denominationalism we often demonize people with whom we disagree. For some reason, we think we have the right to judge someone's heart when we don't agree with his or her core values. I personally don't agree with many of our president's policies, perspectives and moral values as I understand them, but I still honor him as the president of the United States and as a man made in the image of God. And I certainly don't believe he is the Antichrist!

In denominationalism we often demonize people with whom we disagree.

I don't know how we can make judgments about a person's motivations when the media—a source with an agenda—feeds us the only information we have about them. It is important to remember that the media is a multibillion-dollar business that is driven primarily by the entertainment industry and secondarily by political worldview, and finally by the "news." There are thousands of potential stories that could be covered every day. But "news stories" are chosen on the basis of their ability to drive the agencies' ratings, which ultimately translates to advertising dollars. To develop strong opinions about a person's heart through a talk show, newspaper or magazine is irresponsible at best and dangerous at worst.

Secret Agent Man

We must shake off the shackles of denominational mindsets and truly love people regardless of their religious persuasions. This frees the Lord to commission an army of pure-hearted lovers who can display the raw power of God and demonstrate the superior wisdom of another age without manipulation and exploitation. Then He can plant these warriors strategically in the darkest corners of society.

Jesus described it like this: "The kingdom of heaven is like leaven, which a woman took and hid in three pecks of flour until it was all leavened" (Matthew 13:33). Could it be at times that we are actually called to be sheep in wolves' clothing? God wants to knead us into society like leaven. We are His secret agents disguised as doctors, housewives, mechanics, computer programmers, schoolteachers and business managers. We are powerful believers, concealed as everyday people, strategically assigned to serve society while simultaneously destroying the works of the devil. Our very lives are a sign and wonder. Not only do we have the message, but we also are the message. To know us is to love us. We are the fruit of God's love, the manifestation of His Person. To put it in automotive terms, "A great car sells itself."

Let me be clear. I am not talking about cowards who call themselves Christians but are afraid to stand up for Christ; nor am I describing churches that are more sensitive to the will of *unbelievers* who may attend a Sunday service than they are to the Spirit of God moving among them. There are a lot of counterfeit leavens that masquerade as some Kingdom value. Jesus put it this way: "Watch out! Beware of the leaven of the Pharisees and the leaven of Herod" (Mark 8:15). At the root of the religious spirit (the leaven of the Pharisees) and the political spirit (the leaven of Herod) is the fear of man. Fear will never lead us to cultural transformation.

**Not only do we have the message,
but we also are the message.**

Prophetic Mascots

The hidden nature of this epoch season was reemphasized to me recently when I taught at our School of Worship. I was gathering my thoughts as I made my way to the podium, and suddenly I heard the Lord say, "Prophesy to the class before you preach to them."

**The prophetic mascot for this hour is no
longer the eagle; it's the owl.**

"What is the word You want me to share?" I inquired.

"The epoch season has changed and it requires a new proph-etic mascot. The prophetic mascot for this hour is no longer the eagle; it's the owl. The owl is nocturnal, so it is designed to live in the night, see through the darkness and knows who's who. It's the symbol of wisdom, and it feasts on rats, rodents and snakes."

I came to the pulpit and prophesied this word to our students as the class listened intently. Just as I finished my declaration, worship leader Jenn Johnson rushed to the front and excitedly took the microphone. "A student was driving home recently and there was an owl in the middle of the road that wouldn't move. He finally got out of his car, picked it up and brought it home with him," she proclaimed, almost jumping out of her skin. "I just called him, and he is bringing the owl to class today."

It is time for the Body of Christ to carry the Kingdom into the darkest places of society.

It is time for the Body of Christ to carry the Kingdom into the darkest places of society. There is a new God-given ability to see through the gloomy, murky and disgusting evil of people's situations and discover the hidden treasures in the Rahabs of life. Like Rahab of old, who worked as a prostitute but became the great-great-great-great-grandmother of Jesus Christ, there are precious souls, entangled in the sins of life and covered with the mire of shame and guilt, just waiting to be recovered. It's time to join the owl brigade!

The Fall of Babylon

One of the best examples of cultural transformation birthed out of Kingdom core values is in the book of Daniel. Daniel provides a great pattern for us, demonstrating how God leavens society through His secret agents. The king of Babylon, Nebuchadnezzar, destroyed Israel, tore down the Temple of Solomon and took four young teenagers prisoner to serve at his will. But what Nebuchadnezzar didn't realize was that when he arrested Daniel, Shadrach, Meshach and Abednego, God had actually taken Babylon captive.

God's strategic plan for transforming Babylon was initiated when Daniel refused to defile himself with the king's wine and choice food (see Daniel 1:8) and insisted on praying three times a day by kneeling toward Jerusalem (see Daniel 6:10). Shadrach, Meshach and Abednego joined the battle when they stared down the spirit of fear by steadfastly refusing to bow down to Nebuchadnezzar's idol in the face of certain death. This insulated them from the prince of the power of the air that was controlling the minds of most of the Babylonian people. It also inoculated them from the cesspool of carnality.

When God saw that He had people who could not be polluted by the evil system around them, He kneaded them into the culture, like leaven into dough, by disguising His four superheroes as magicians and conjurers (see Daniel 1:20). They customized their life to meet the needs of an evil empire without compromising their character. They were so assimilated into the Babylonian culture that they even took on the names of the Babylonian gods. Daniel's name was changed to Belteshazzar, which was the name of Nebuchadnezzar's god (see Daniel 4:8). Systematically and strategically, these boys began to leverage their Kingdom influence into the hearts of the Babylonians and Persians. Over a period of 70 years these guys dismantled and displaced the powers of darkness by demonstrating the power and wisdom of a superior kingdom. Finally, the Persian king, Cyrus, released the people of God to rebuild

Jerusalem and restore the Israelites to their land. He even funded the multimillion-dollar Temple project.

Human Rights

King Cyrus the Great was the last in a long line of rulers that Daniel served. Although Daniel was quite old when he worked for Cyrus, his influence on the king might well be his greatest legacy. You see, not only is Cyrus the Great credited with the release and restoration of the Israelis, but he is also the father of the concept of human rights! Twenty-five hundred years ago, King Cyrus authored a human rights scroll that has become the prototype for the United Nations.[3] Literally billons of people owe their freedom and equality to a Persian king whose rule was prophesied by Isaiah years before he was born (see Isaiah 45:1-7). This extraordinary man was guarded by angels and mentored by Daniel (see Ezra 1:1; Daniel 10-12). I guess you just really never know who is growing up in your house.

> **I guess you just really never know who is growing up in your house.**

From the opening scene of the story, these guys' superior character, supernatural powers and extraordinary love continually exposed the Babylonians and the Persian kingdom to another realm. This is the kind of leaven God intends for us to be on the earth—hidden superheroes destroying evil fortresses, influencing kings and making disciples out of every nation! The handwriting is on the wall. God has numbered the devil's kingdom and put an end to it. He has weighed it on the scales and found it deficient. He has handed the world over to the sons of light (see Daniel 5:25-28).

God wants to hide His leaven in every part of society. Not all of us are going to be assigned to palaces to influence the kings of our day. But in whatever sphere of influence God puts us, we are called to *lead* by putting the superior qualities of the Kingdom on display—the virtues of integrity, honor, compassion, service, power, wisdom and courage.

The other dynamic that is important for us to consider here is that whatever ground we take by force we will have to maintain through force. But whatever position we gain through honor will be protected by favor.

Whatever position we gain through honor will be protected by favor.

Discipling Nations

The Body of Christ so desperately needs to learn how to influence society in such a way that people are drawn to us. We have the answers to the world's problems, but we are fumbling our God-given assignment. Our failure to disciple nations is largely a manifestation of our lack of understanding of how to bring true transformation to the lives of people, especially to those who aren't hungry for it yet.

Jesus commissioned us to *make* disciples of *all* nations and then *teach* them (see Matthew 28:18-20). The Greek word for disciple, *mathetes,* means learner. It may surprise some leaders that we are responsible to *create learners* and then to *teach them*! I have heard many leaders say things like, "People are just not hungry for the truth." What these leaders don't realize is that we are responsible to motivate people to want to learn, receive and grow so that we can teach, equip and train them. Most of us have had an important person in our life who was so passionate about a particular subject that he or she inspired that interest in us and caused us to hunger to know more. This is what we are called to do for *all* the nations of the world.

**We are responsible to *create learners*
and then to *teach them*!**

As I pointed out earlier, Jesus sent us out as sheep among wolves. The world is hungry for the Body of Christ. They want to consume us. But they need a taste test, a little nibble of the real thing so that they can become hungry enough to "eat His flesh and drink His blood" (see John 6:54). When Jesus told people that they must eat His flesh and drink His blood, He wasn't talking about cannibalism. He was referring to ingesting the Living Word of God. Christ is the Word that became flesh. It is important that we encourage people to ingest Jesus and digest His life until Christ is literally formed in them. There is an old saying that is true in this case: *You are what you eat!*

Much of the world has ingested the Bible in one form or another, but many have never digested the living, active Word of God. Religion temporarily filled their souls, but it never satisfied their longing for real life. The world has had its fill of religion and is fed up with it.

**Transformation requires assimilation,
not just consumption.**

Transformation requires assimilation, not just consumption. For the time being, I am lactose intolerant. When I consume dairy products, my body will not assimilate them into my system. Many people in the world are gospel intolerant. When they listen to the preaching of the Word, it has no effect on them, or worse yet, it actually creates a negative reaction in some of them. And then there are others who have consumed just enough religion that they have become inoculated from the real Jesus. Hearing about the Bible without experiencing God leads to religious form without any power (see 2 Timothy 3:5). It is like exchanging the Communion meal for a dinner commentary or a cookbook.

It is time to become as wise as serpents.

We owe the world an encounter with God Himself. When people get exposed to their Creator, they find Him enticing—I mean, simply irresistible. We need a strategic plan birthed by the Holy Spirit (a "spirategy") that can bring the Kingdom into every realm of society. We have emphasized the "innocent as doves" part for decades. While holding to this, it is time to become as wise as serpents (see Matthew 10:16).

Standing at the Threshold of History

In May 2009, God gave me a profound prophetic word. He said that He gave a man a network of churches (God told me the man's name, but I don't want to dishonor him by revealing it here) that became a catalyst for a worldwide movement. The movement became so large and powerful that it began to redefine its fellowship of churches. The leadership of the church network had to decide if they were going to protect their identity or embrace the movement. They chose to protect the fellowship of churches and they cut off the movement.

The Early Church

In Acts chapter 15, the same scenario was taking place. The mother church in Jerusalem, which was basically Judaism in practice, with Jesus and the Holy Spirit taking center stage, was growing and suddenly jumped the firewall of religious tradition, enveloping the Gentiles. The Church became a catalyst to a movement because, of course, there were many more Gentiles than there were Jews. But to make matters even more complicated, the Gentiles who were getting saved were steeped in Greek mythology and polytheism (the worship of many gods). Most of them knew nothing of the Old Testament—the stories of creation, the flood, and so forth—or people like Abraham, Isaac, Jacob, Moses, Esther and David. Therefore, as these Gentiles came into the Kingdom, they began to dramatically redefine the Church.

The apostles called for a leadership summit in Jerusalem to decide what to do. The multitudes listened as the most powerful church leaders in the world wrestled over this dilemma. The discussion began with Paul and Barnabas sharing their incredible stories of God's supernatural intervention in the lives of the Gentiles. Peter followed with his miraculous testimonies of God filling the Gentiles with the Holy Spirit. God was redeeming them in the same way He had saved the Jews, in spite of the fact that they were not keeping all the religious traditions, rules and laws.

The apostles had to decide if they were going to let the movement redefine the Church as they knew it, or if they were going to cut off the movement to protect the Jewish identity of the Body. They listened to the Holy Spirit and chose to embrace the movement (see Acts 15:28). James made this historic statement about the Gentile church: "It is my judgment that we do not trouble those who are turning to God from among the Gentiles, but that we write to them that they abstain from things contaminated by idols and from fornication and from what is strangled and from blood" (Acts 15:19-20). A letter followed releasing the Gentiles from having to observe Mosaic Law and Jewish tradition, and the rest is history! From that point on, the gospel continued to spread more powerfully among the Gentiles until there were very few Jewish Christians by A.D. 100.

Standing at the Same Threshold

In the Word I received about the man who received a network of churches, the Lord told me that as a Church we are standing at that same threshold in history once again. There's about to be a massive harvest that will be coming from a relatively unreached people group. They will know nothing about the traditions of religion or the foundations of Church history. The Bible itself will be foreign to them, yet the Holy Spirit is going to fall on them in droves. We will be confronted with the same decision that our forefathers faced: Will we cut off the movement to save the Church's identity and reputation, or will we embrace the movement at the risk of being misunderstood by the religious community?

As we cross this historic threshold, it's important to remind ourselves that 2,000 years ago our Lord paved the way into this divine paradox. The company He kept seemed to redefine Him to the religious community. They labeled Him a "drunkard" and a "friend of sinners." Religion always seems to find a way to isolate us from the people who need God the most. But we must brave the storms of reputation and reach into the cesspools of darkness, dirtying our hands with the unredeemed souls of men and women.

We must brave the storms of reputation and reach into the cesspools of darkness, dirtying our hands with the souls of men.

Notes

1. Mark Haefeli, director, *Paul McCartney in Red Square: A Concert Film* (A&E Home Video, 2003).
2. Jennifer Robison, "What Percentage of the Population Is Gay," Gallup, October 8, 2002. www.gallup.co/poll/6961/what-percentage-population-gay.aspx.
3. "Cyrus Charter of the Human Rights Cylinder: First Charter of Human Rights," Farsinet. http://www.farsinet.com/cyrus/.

4

Unreasonable Courage

*The difference between those who do
something and those who don't is that those
who do something . . . do something!*
BANNING LIEBSCHER

The Tipping Point

It is important for us to realize that along with apostolic mantles and strategic missions, it will also take unreasonable
courage to break out of the secure prison of powerless religion
and the mindless thinking of the crowd to move into the pre-
vailing place of global influence.

Living in a crowd directly affects our ability to take courage
and responsibility to act. In his best-selling book *The Tipping
Point*, Malcolm Gladwell recounts the now classic story of
mindless crowd-think revealed in the report of a young woman
named Kitty Genovese, who was brutally raped and murdered
in 1964, in Queens, New York. The most shocking part of the
story was that, according to the *New York Times* report, 38 of
her neighbors witnessed Genovese as she desperately fought for
her life. Though the incident lasted more than half an hour,
not one of them intervened or *even called the police*.

This report provoked various investigations into what two scientists termed the "bystander problem." Their studies revealed that if one person witnesses a crime, it is likely that he or she will get involved. But as the number of witnesses grows, the chances of intervention drastically decrease. The apparent reason for this is that "when people are in a group . . . responsibility for acting is diffused."[1] Everyone thinks that everyone else has made the call, and consequently, no one does anything!

Former president Ronald Reagan famously said, "To sit back hoping that someday, some way, someone will make things right, is to go on feeding the crocodile, hoping he will eat you last . . . but eat you he will." When we choose not to make that 911 call, we had better remind ourselves that we may become the next victim!

Like Sheep We Go Astray

The Bible addresses this social dynamic when it says, "All of us like sheep have gone astray" (Isaiah 53:6; see also 1 Peter 2:25). It doesn't say like wolves; it says sheep. How do sheep go astray? They spend all their time watching each other's butts, hoping that there is a shepherd in front of the flock somewhere.

We all suffer from this ultimate crowd deception at times. We get so used to the scenery that we develop a strange security in rump watching. Heck, the motion itself is mesmerizing. It's a career opportunity for some; for others it's a hobby like bird watching. You can always recognize the rump watchers, because they're saying things like, "Well gosh, Mildred, we must be going the right way. Look at all those butts ahead of us. I mean, gol-ly, all those butts can't be wrong, can they?" I know the prophet Chiquita said, "The banana that leaves the bunch is the one that gets eaten." But for crying out loud, can we learn to think a little, please?

═══════════════════════════════

> For crying out loud, can we learn
> to think a little, please?

═══════════════════════════════

Monkey Business

When people stop thinking for themselves, they cut off the flow of invention, innovation and advancement. This creates a stale culture where traditions and rituals lose their significance, mostly because no one can remember why the heck they are doing them.

This reminds me of the "five monkey" experiment I heard about a couple years ago. The experiment starts with a cage containing five monkeys. Inside the cage there is a banana on a string and a set of stairs under it. Before long, a monkey goes to the stairs and starts to climb toward the banana. As soon as he touches the stairs, all of the other monkeys are sprayed with cold water. After a while, another monkey makes an attempt with the same result—the other monkeys are sprayed with cold water. Pretty soon, when another monkey tries to get the banana, the other monkeys try to prevent the monkey from doing so.

Eventually, the cold water is removed, along with one of the monkeys, which is replaced with a new monkey. The new monkey sees the banana and goes to climb the stairs. To the new monkey's horror, the other monkeys attack it. After another attempt, it knows if it touches the stairs, it will be assaulted.

Next, another of the original five monkeys is removed and replaced with a new one. The newcomer goes to the stairs and is attacked. The previous newcomer joins in the punishment with enthusiasm! Then, a third monkey is replaced with a new one, then a fourth, and then the fifth. Every time a newcomer takes to the stairs, it is attacked.

By this point, most of the monkeys beating the new monkey have no idea why they were not permitted to climb the stairs or why they are participating in the beating. After replacing all the original monkeys, none of the remaining monkeys has ever been sprayed with cold water. Still, no monkey ever again approaches the stairs. Why not, you may ask? Because as far as they know, "That's the way it's always been done around here!"

It's time to question reality. It's important to ask ourselves why we do the things we do. Is it possible that the conditions that caused us to keep certain important traditions have changed? Has deeper revelation or new technology made the customs in which we take so much pride and from which we get so much comfort irrelevant? It's time that we transition from a stereotype to a prototype.

**It's time to question reality.
It's time that we transition from a stereotype
to a prototype.**

I Have Decided

I have decided to think for myself. I am not rebellious or independent, nor do I want to reinvent the wheel, so to speak. But I will not let Rush Limbaugh, Sean Hannity, Piers Morgan, Ed Schultz, Bill O' Reilly or anyone else, for that matter, think for me. It is not that I don't appreciate other people's opinions. I really do learn a lot from others. It's just that I am no one's puppet. I have been commanded to arise and *shine*, not arise and *reflect* (see Isaiah 60:1). I have been called to be a voice, not an echo. I refuse to be reduced to a political affiliation, a denomination, a generation, a geographic location, my sexual orientation or my ordination. I will not settle for becoming a cheap imitation of another instead of an original of myself. I won't be condensed to a history lesson, nor will I allow someone's fear to constrain my own exploits. I will not bow down to anyone's idol or be conformed to old religious ideologies that will render me irrelevant to the Kingdom.

I have been commanded to arise and shine, not arise and reflect.

On the other hand, it is not my desire to become a maverick or a heretic who exchanges the solid foundation of time-tested truth for the test tube of isolation. Therefore, I will allow the Holy Spirit to lead me, guide me and correct me. I will submit to true leadership and remain moldable, teachable and humble. I will love passionately, live zealously, work wholeheartedly, laugh joyfully and be completely spent at the end of my life. I will walk powerfully, pray unceasingly, give extravagantly and serve God with my whole being.

Expert Advice

It takes courage to break ranks with religious clones and think for ourselves. But we must realize that creativity, imagination and real learning are never cultivated in crowds. We also have to recognize that there are no permanent "arrivals" or plateaus in this life. Either we are growing, expanding and developing, or we are declining, growing stagnant and petrifying. No matter how much you have seen, experienced and learned, there is always more, always a new frontier that requires courage to explore. If you stop living on this edge of continuous growth and expansion, you risk cutting yourself off from your potential in God.

What you know can keep you from what you need to know.

Bill Johnson says, "What you know can keep you from what you need to know." He's right, because as soon as you consider yourself an expert, you stop learning and growing. The Pharisees are a great example of people who memorized the Word of God and didn't recognize the author of the Book when He stood right in front of them explaining the Book to them. History is full of experts whose imagination was imprisoned by their education, experience or fear of rejection. Consider some of the following examples:

- "Man will never reach the moon regardless of all future scientific advances." (Dr. Lee DeForest, father of radio and grandfather of television)
- "The bomb will never go off. I speak as an expert in explosives." (Admiral William Leahy, U.S. Atomic Bomb Project)
- "There is no likelihood man can ever tap the power of the atom." (Robert Millikan, Nobel Prize in physics, 1923)
- "Computers in the future may weigh no more than 1.5 tons." (*Popular Mechanics*, 1949)

- "I think there is a world market for maybe five computers." (Thomas Watson, chairman of IBM, 1943)
- "I have traveled the length and breadth of this country and talked with the best people, and I can assure you that data processing is a fad that won't last out the year." (Editor in charge of business books for Prentice Hall, 1957)
- "But what is it good for?" (Engineer at the Advanced Computing Systems Division of IBM, commenting on the microchip, 1968)
- "640K ought to be enough for anybody." (Bill Gates, 1981)
- "This 'telephone' has too many shortcomings to be seriously considered as a means of communication. The device is inherently of no value to us." (Western Union internal memo, 1876)
- "The wireless music box has no imaginable commercial value. Who would pay for a message sent to nobody in particular?" (David Sarnoff Associates, response to urgings for investment in radio, 1920s)
- "The concept is interesting and well formed, but in order to earn better than a 'C', the idea must be feasible." (Yale University management professor, in response to Fred Smith's paper proposing reliable overnight delivery service. Smith went on to found the Federal Express Corporation.)
- "I'm just glad it'll be Clark Gable who falls on his face, not Gary Cooper." (Gary Cooper, on his decision not to take the leading role in *Gone with the Wind*)
- "A cookie store is a bad idea. Besides, the market research reports say America likes crispy cookies, not soft and chewy cookies like you make." (Response to Debbi Fields' idea of starting Mrs. Field's Cookies)

- "We don't like their sound, and guitar music is on the way out." (Decca Recording Company, rejecting the Beatles, 1962)
- "Heavier-than-air flying machines are impossible." (Lord Kelvin, president of the Royal Society, 1895)
- "Drill for oil? You mean drill into the ground to try and find oil? You're crazy!" (Drillers that Edwin L. Drake tried to enlist to his project to drill for oil, 1859)
- "Airplanes are interesting toys but of no military value." (Marechal Ferdinand Foch, Professor of Strategy, École Supérieure de Guerre, France)
- "Everything that can be invented has been invented." (Charles H. Duell, Commissioner, U.S. Office of Patents, 1899)
- "The super computer is technologically impossible. It would take all of the water that flows over Niagara Falls to cool the heat generated by the number of vacuum tubes required." (Professor of Electrical Engineering, New York University)
- "I don't know what use anyone could find for a machine that would make copies of documents. It certainly couldn't be a feasible business by itself." (Head of IBM, refusing to back the idea, forcing the inventor to found Xerox)
- "Louis Pasteur's theory of germs is ridiculous fiction." (Pierre Packet, Professor of Physiology at Toulouse, France, 1872)
- "The abdomen, the chest, and the brain will forever be shut from the intrusion of the wise and humane surgeon." (Sir John Eric Ericksen, British surgeon, appointed Surgeon-Extraordinary to Queen Victoria, 1873)
- "There is no reason anyone would want a computer in their home." (Ken Olson, president, chairman, founder of Digital Equipment Corp., 1977)[2]

Where would we be today if people always let the "experts" dictate the boundaries of their imagination? How different would society be if these history makers had followed the crowd or allowed their ideas to be judged in the courtroom of popular opinion? It takes a deep thinker to realize there are eggs that were meant to fly!

The Four-Minute Mile

On May 6, 1954, Roger Bannister broke the four-minute mile. Until he did, the four-minute mile was considered not merely unreachable but, according to physiologists of the time, "dangerous to the health of any athlete who attempted to reach it." Scientists told runners that it was physically impossible to run a mile in under four minutes. As a result, for thousands of years no athletes ever ran a mile in under four minutes. When Bannister crossed the finish line in 3 minutes, 59.4 seconds, he broke through the veil of the impossible. Six weeks later, on June 21, 1954, John Landy broke Bannister's record. By 1957, 16 other runners had broken the four-minute mile.

**Often the difference between what is
and what could be is not measured by
the length of the track, but rather by
the resistance between our ears.**

So what happened to the *physical* barrier that prevented humans from running a mile in under four minutes? Was there a sudden leap in human evolution? No. It was the *change in thinking* that made the difference. Bannister proved that it was possible to break the four-minute mile.

Often the difference between what is and what could be is not measured by the length of the track, but rather by the resistance between our ears. The impossible barriers we perceive are frequently just obstacles in our own minds. Previous runners had been held back by their belief system and mindset. When the spell was finally broken, 16 other runners saw that it was possible and went on to do the same thing. Since then, hundreds of athletes have broken the four-minute mile. One man had a showdown with fear and gunned it down on the streets of mediocrity. More than five decades later, people are still feeling the effects of his courage.

One man had a showdown with fear and gunned it down on the streets of mediocrity.

One City

It is astounding to me that one person's breakthrough can have such a powerful ripple effect in the sea of humanity. Bill Johnson had an experience several years ago that proved to me that Roger Bannister was more than a great athlete; he was a prophetic symbol of the way God wanted to transform cities. Bill went to an all-day prayer meeting in Vacaville, California, which is about two hours from Redding. The event was already in session when Bill arrived, so he settled into a place to pray with the other intercessors as they stormed heaven for earth's reformation. After some time, a well-known prophet approached Bill with a prophetic word.

He said, "Bill, I believe that God is looking for one city that would be completely His. God wants to cause a breakthrough in one city that affects every realm of society. When that one city falls under the power of God, it will create a domino effect across the entire world that will result in city after city being brought into the Kingdom."

"I believe that city is Redding, California!" Bill responded.

A few minutes later, another seasoned prophetess came to Bill and whispered in his ear, "Bill, I think that God is looking for one city that would be completely His. If God finds one city that welcomes His presence in every place in society, it will cause a domino effect and hundreds of cities all around the world will come into the Kingdom."

Bill started to say, "I believe—" but before he could finish, she interrupted, "I believe that city is Redding!"

Could Redding, or your city, be the tipping point of historic exploits?

Could Redding, or your city, be the tipping point of historic exploits? Is it possible that one city could break the barrier of naysayers and doubters like Roger Bannister did the four-minute mile? Will history record a massive global revival that dramatically lowers the crime rate to the point where children can play in the streets at night again, reduces the divorce statistic, causes cancer to be spoken of in the past tense like smallpox and so stimulates the economy through generosity that there is literally no poor among us? Could the transformation go so deep and be so broad that joy fills every home; people stop abusing their children; immoral businesses like drugs and pornography dry up; and abortion is considered a barbaric, inhumane act like cannibalism?

What if signs and wonders became so frequent that God's glory literally hovered over cities like a mist and "sinners" became a minority ethnic group? We believe that Redding is destined to fulfill all of these dreams, and we are praying, working and living to that end. To borrow a line from John Lennon, "You may say that I'm a dreamer, but I am not the only one."[3] Maybe someday you will join us and the world will live *and be won* (my play on words).

Democracies Rule?

Democratic culture perpetuates the illusion that it isn't the Roger Bannisters of the world that create breakthroughs, but the crowd that is most often right. The masses rule, and the will of the majority determine history. But as Malcolm Gladwell so profoundly pointed out with the true illustration of a witnessed crime where no one came forward to help, crowds rarely act. Mobs become swamps: stale, murky waters of inaction.

Mobs become swamps: stale, murky waters of inaction.

Believers who grow up in democratic countries often live under the delusion that the Kingdom is a democracy. We forget that God refers to Himself as King, not President. For example, we think that if we can rally a million people to pray in Washington, DC, then certainly God will have to move on behalf of our nation. I personally love to see Christians get together for anything, and I support large gatherings, but the kingdom of God isn't a democracy; it is a theocracy.

When Judah was in trouble, God commanded the prophet Jeremiah, "Roam to and fro through the streets of Jerusalem, and look now and take note. And seek in her open squares, if you can find *a man*, if there *is one* who does justice, who seeks truth, then I will pardon her" (Jeremiah 5:1, emphasis added). The majority doesn't rule in the natural world, as we saw in the previous chapter with the example of the gay community, and God isn't moved by the masses in the unseen realm either. The Lord doesn't look down from heaven and take a head count to see who is on the side of a particular issue so that He can act. Believe it or not, He is not the cosmic pollster! Can you imagine Jesus saying to Gabriel, "Well, Gabe, it looks like we finally got a majority of believers to agree with us on that marriage issue. You can go ahead and intervene on that thing now"? That's ridiculous, but it is the predominant mindset of the Church.

God continues to say, as He has always said, "Find me a man, a woman, a son, or a daughter. Just find me someone who is fed up, fired up, and filled up." God told the Israelites, "The eyes of the Lord move to and fro throughout the earth that He may strongly support those whose heart is completely His" (2 Chronicles 16:9). God isn't looking for a crowd—He is longing for a person! He isn't wowed by the masses or mesmerized by the multitudes. Neither is He put off by the powerless. He just needs someone to step out of the crowd and make that phone call. He is simply longing once again for a person like David to emerge from the wilderness and let the giants of life know that they have *messed with the wrong guy. They have taunted the armies of the living God.*

Movements

Despite popular opinion, movements never define people. Men and women define movements! In 1955, a 42-year-old Southern black woman, exhausted from a hard day at work, refused to sit in the back of a transit bus. The bus driver warned her that her defiance would be cause for him to call the police and have her arrested. But she had had enough of white bigotry. She knew that as long as she submitted to it, she was allowing injustice to continue. She bravely did the right thing and faced the consequences. Her name was Rosa Parks. Rosa stepped out of the crowd and made the call. She wasn't a part of a movement. There was no movement. Instead, Ms. Parks put her shoulder into the boulder of history, gave it a shove and history not only moved—it is still moving! Later in life, Rosa wrote, "Without a vision the people perish, but without courage dreams die."

When a young preacher named Dr. Martin Luther King got involved in the civil rights movement, he wanted to create a peaceful revolution. People told him he was crazy. They said there was no such thing as social change without acts of violence. Dr. King refused to listen to them. A while later, some radical white supremacists bombed his house. He was home with his wife and young daughter when the explosion went off. The blast ripped through their house, tearing off its entire front, narrowly missing his family. Within minutes, angry black militants arrived and tried to convince Dr. King to fight back with violence. But he stood on the rubble of what was once his front porch and proclaimed forgiveness for the perpetrators. The rest is history: a man, a dream, and his God. We need to be like Winston Churchill, who said, "History will be kind to me, for I intend to write it!"

Inventory Your Strength

One of the main reasons people don't act is because of an overwhelming sense of inadequacy. It is so easy to inventory our weaknesses and disqualify ourselves from the historic exploits God has assigned to each of us. We forget that Jesus borrowed a couple of fish and some bread from a boy's lunch box and fed a multitude (see Matthew 14:15-20). The crowd didn't eat rice and beans, because the boy brought fish and loaves. Jesus multiplied what the boy had, not what he didn't have. God doesn't care about what you don't have. He only cares about what you do have!

It is so easy to inventory our weaknesses and disqualify ourselves from the historic exploits God has assigned to each of us.

Many people try to tell God why they can't carry out their divine mission. They say things like, "I am too old, too young, too dumb, too ugly, too uneducated, too weird or too weak. I was born into the wrong family. I was a prostitute, a thief, a murderer or an adulteress. I've been divorced. I have had an abortion, or several." The list goes on and on. Take courage, folks—you are among great company. Life is filled with history makers like us!

If you think you're too dumb, remember Samson (see Judges 13–16). Now, that guy was dumb! I mean, come on—when your girlfriend ties you up three times and tells you that your enemy is after you and you still spill the beans, that's an IQ crisis. Yet, in the end, his greatest victory followed his greatest defeat.

Perhaps you think you are too young to make a difference. At eight years old, Josiah was too young to cross the street by himself, much less be king. And talk about generational curses— Josiah's grandfather was Manasseh, the wickedest king in Israel's history; and his father was Amon, who walked in all the ways of Manasseh. Yikes! Yet Josiah led Judah into one of its greatest revivals and brought his whole nation back to God (see 2 Kings 22–23).

Maybe you are just plain strange. Join the exalted ranks of John the Baptist. The man was weird. He wore an outfit that never was or ever has been in style. And he ate locusts—you can't even order those things at the finest restaurants. Yet Jesus said no one greater than John had ever been born.

Ah, I get it: you have some sexual hang-ups. Tell your troubles to Rahab, the prostitute who helped Joshua conquer the Promised Land and later wound up as the great-great-great-grandmother of Jesus Christ (see Joshua 2; 6; Matthew 1:5).

So you're an ex-con. How about the "man after God's heart" named David, who committed adultery and then murdered the woman's husband (see 2 Samuel 11)?

Oh, you have a drinking problem. Noah, who courageously obeyed God and partnered with Him to save the entire human race, got so drunk that he took all his clothes off (see Genesis 9:20-21). Just a minor issue . . . *not!*

God is famous for accomplishing extraordinary things with ordinary people.

You think you are too ugly to make a difference. Have you ever seen a picture of Abraham Lincoln? Now that dude was ugly. He was so ugly that a 10-year-old girl met him on the campaign trail and said, "Mister Lincoln, you are so ugly that you should grow a beard to cover up your face." So he did! Yet that ugly man became one of our greatest presidents and saved our nation from the tyranny of slavery.

Maybe you have some emotional challenges. Winston Churchill (who looked like Mister Peabody, by the way) had what he called his "black dog." The "dog" was his struggle with depression that kept him in bed for up to 30 days at a time. Many historians believe Churchill was mentally ill. If so, he did more while mentally ill than most people do in their healthy state of mind.

So you never finished high school. Peter's claim to fame is that his messages were profound so they had to be from God, because the guy had no education (see Acts 4:13). The stories go on and on. What is your excuse for not fulfilling your call? Get over it! God is famous for accomplishing extraordinary things with ordinary people.

There are many people who call themselves leaders but are actually just puppets of the masses.

Braveheart

There are many people who call themselves leaders but are actually just puppets of the masses. Their strings are pulled by popular opinion as they search for the path of least resistance. Their goal is to make decisions that please as many people as possible. But what they refuse to understand is that when you fear the people, you are not leading them; they are leading you. It is important to realize that the organizations we are called to lead can become idols, something we bow down to instead of serve and lead. Jack Taylor put it this way: "An idol is something you have to check with before you say yes to God." It is so easy to find ourselves bowing to the will of the crowd instead of following the cloud of God's direction.

An idol is something you have to check with before you say yes to God.

In the movie *Braveheart*, William Wallace tries to convince Robert the Bruce to join his tattered army of makeshift soldiers in freeing Scotland from the tyranny of the English. Bruce argues with William and tries to persuade him to calm down. Finally, in a rage, Wallace storms out of the castle with Robert the Bruce in pursuit, still trying to convince him to compromise with his enemies and make peace with England.

William Wallace stops abruptly on the castle steps and turns to Robert the Bruce. The camera zooms in on the two men as they stand there, staring into each other's eyes for what seems like an eternity. Then, in his best Scottish accent, William delivers the most powerful lines of the entire movie: "Men don't follow titles, they follow courage! If you lead them, they will follow you. It's true, you know. I can see it in your eyes!"

Men don't follow titles, they follow courage!

I understand this is just a line in a movie, but it's still true. In this hour, when the political spirit seems to reign supreme and the media high priesthood crucifies anyone who disagrees with the crowd, God is still searching for a man, for a woman, for somebody who has the courage to stand with Him. He just needs a person who will truly lead, make the call and lift up a cry for righteousness—someone who will be a voice for the Kingdom, not just an echo of past religious ideologies or some political clone, chameleons whose convictions change with the company they keep.

> **Courage inspires people. It's the bridge between what is and what should be.**

John Maxwell says, "When leaders lack confidence, their followers lack commitment." Courage inspires people. It's the bridge between what is and what should be.

> **Until we have something to die for, we really never live.**

Dying to Live

Until we have something to die for, we really never live. Jesus put it best: "For whoever wishes to save his life will lose it; but whoever loses his life for My sake will find it" (Matthew 16:25). Everyone's life is terminal! We are all going to die; we just don't know when. The real question is, will we really ever live? I am not talking about taking up space and sucking up air; I mean really living, making a difference, pushing past our fear and taking hold of our destiny. Until we deal with death, we don't really ever live. The writer of Hebrews put it this way:

Therefore, since the children share in flesh and blood, He Himself likewise also partook of the same, that through death He might render powerless him who had the power of death, that is, the devil, and might free those who through fear of death were subject to slavery all their lives (Hebrews 2:14-15).

It is only when we deal with the inevitable that we can actually do the impossible. When a person loses the fear of death, he or she begins to move into new realms of impact.

It is only when we deal with the inevitable that we can actually do the impossible.

According to an ancient Roman adage, *A coward dies a thousand deaths, but a brave man dies only once!* Fear will rob us of life every day. The life we were called to live lies on the other side of our fears. Remember, God didn't childproof the Garden. He isn't as interested in keeping us safe as He is in trying to keep us from a meaningless life. Courage is a catalyst to great leadership and a life full of purpose.

Courageous Love

In September 2005, a couple of young people came to Bethel's ministry school. Kerstin was from Switzerland, and Tyson was an American. They fell in love, and it wasn't long before they were married. They so adored each other that watching them interact was like imagining a scene out of a romantic novel. Soon Kerstin was pregnant with their first child and their life took on an ecstatic joy that I have rarely ever observed. That same year, Kerstin won our school's highest honor, the M. Earl Johnson Award, which is only given to two students per class for their outstanding character, achievement and anointing. Kerstin and Tyson were on top of the world, and we were all being pulled along in the wake of their elation.

Then suddenly something terrible happened. Four months into Kerstin's pregnancy, she returned from the doctor with a serious report of stage-four cancer that had spread through most of her body. She was rushed to a specialist, who confirmed her condition. The doctors felt confident they could save her life if she began treatment immediately, but explained that the chemotherapy would kill the baby. The choice was clear—either abort the baby and live, or carry the child to full term and die. Kerstin didn't hesitate; her mind was made up. She would give up her life to save her child if necessary. Five months later, a healthy baby boy named Kalani came into the world to two very excited parents. Kalani means "heavenly," and he was certainly a gift from God. In the meantime, our church prayed, fasted and warred over her condition. But 10 months after the heavenly child was born, his earthly mother was gone!

Most people spend their existence trying to save their life, wondering why they are never really fulfilled. Maybe Mick Jagger said it best when he sang, "I can't get no . . . satisfaction."[4] But Kerstin had the courage to lay down her life so that someone else would live. Do you?

Alexander the Great

This courage to die for something has always been a vital ingredient in any history-making endeavor. Alexander the Great is one of the classic examples of a leader who inspired people to give their lives for something greater than themselves. A few centuries before Christ, Alexander conquered most of the known world with his military strength. One day, Alexander and a small company of soldiers approached a strongly defended, walled city. Alexander, standing outside the walls, raised his voice, demanding to see the king. The king, standing on the battlements above the invading army, agreed to hear Alexander's demands.

"Surrender to me immediately," commanded Alexander.

The king laughed. "Why should I surrender to you? We have you far outnumbered. You are no threat to us!"

Alexander replied confidently, "Allow me to demonstrate why you should surrender."

Alexander ordered his men to line up in single file and start marching. He marched them straight toward a sheer cliff that dropped hundreds of feet to rocks below. The king and his soldiers watched in shocked disbelief as, one by one, Alexander's soldiers marched without hesitation right off the cliff to their deaths. After 10 soldiers had died, Alexander ordered the rest of his men to stop and return to his side. The king and his soldiers surrendered on the spot to Alexander the Great.

Masquerade

There are so many things in life that masquerade as courage but are really just fear dressed up in a valor costume. When folks make comments like, "I don't care what people think of me," they are deceiving themselves. Everybody needs affection and encouragement from others. It's just human nature. The real issue with these people is that they are afraid that if others get to know them, they won't like them. Therefore, they work hard to reject others before they have a chance to be rejected.

Then there are the "I do all the talking" fear folks. Have you ever had a conversation with someone who won't let you get a word in edgewise? These people are terrified of being controlled by others, so they won't let anyone speak into their lives.

There are so many things in life that masquerade as courage but are really just fear dressed up in a valor costume.

How about the rageaholic? He stays mad so he doesn't have to be fearful.

There's the seductive woman or the beauty queen who is frightened by men and has learned how to use her body to reduce aggressive lions to purring pussycats.

There is the brainiac who needs to be smarter than everyone else to deal with his insecurities. He believes as long as he can out-think everyone on the planet, he won't have to be afraid of them.

The bodybuilder can be using another fear crutch, dealing with his or her trepidation by being stronger than everyone else.

Ever met the Bible scholar guy? He knows everything about the Book and hides behind religion.

The list could go on and on. I am not suggesting in any way that beauty, brains, talent or muscles are wrong in themselves (rage is an exception, of course). But when we are motivated out of fear instead of inspired by faith, the wrong spirit anoints our strengths.

Courageous Types

There are two types of courage that are admired in the kingdom of God. The first one I call the "fear that has said its prayers" kind of courage. It is courage that takes action in the midst of intense fear. Esther demonstrated this class of courage. Haman, the king's right-hand man, hated a Jewish man named Mordecai because he refused to treat him like a god. In revenge, Haman convinced the king to exterminate all of the Jews, not knowing the queen herself was Jewish.

Queen Esther was stressed out, but she refused to let her fear dictate her future.

Mordecai was Queen Esther's cousin, and was responsible for her becoming queen in the first place. Mordecai discovered Haman's genocide plot and came to the king's gate, dressed in sackcloth, and mourning and wailing. Troubled and scared, Esther tried to calm him down and get him to change his clothes. This is where the plot thickens. Mordecai brought Esther to the point of action with these famous words:

> Do not imagine that you in the king's palace can escape any more than all the Jews. For if you remain silent at this time, relief and deliverance will arise for the Jews from another place and you and your father's house will perish. And who knows whether you have not attained royalty for such a time as this? (Esther 4:13-14).

After this, Esther sent a message in reply to Mordecai, saying, "Go, assemble all the Jews who are found in Susa, and fast for me; do not eat or drink for three days, night or day. I and my maidens also will fast in the same way. And thus I will go in to the king, which is not according to the law; and if I perish, I perish" (Esther 4:16).

Queen Esther was stressed out, but she refused to let her fear dictate her future. She entered the palace and appealed to her king. She won the king's favor, and he hung Haman on the gallows that Haman had erected for Mordecai. Esther rescued the Jews and saved the day.

The dogs of doom often stand at the doors of our destiny. They start barking when we are about to cross the threshold of our God-given purpose. Most people never fully enter into their promised land because they allow fear to dictate the boundaries of their future. They reduce their lives to accommodate the dogs and mistake the silence for peace. For example, if you are so afraid to fly that you never get on a plane, you won't feel scared because you have scaled back your life to silence the dogs. You may think you are absolutely tranquil, but the truth is that you are still full of fear. Subconsciously, you know that flying will awaken the sleeping monster, and he will torment you until you slay him or obey him.

Slaying Dragons

These fear dragons have wandered the earth, tormenting people for generations. It was these same fearmongers who thousands of years ago kept the children of Israel out of the land that God had promised them. There are always giants waiting for us at the border of our destiny, because we need them! The process of conquering them is what prepares us to prosper in the Promised Land.

It is fear-and-trembling courage that moves us past the Goliaths of our life. The great apostle Paul, who courageously endured imprisonment, stoning, beatings and shipwreck was left for dead on at least one occasion, and was finally beheaded. He told the Corinthians, "I was with you in weakness and in fear and in much trembling" (1 Corinthians 2:3). Later he wrote these words to the believers at Philippi: "So then, my beloved, just as you have always obeyed, not as in my presence only, but now much more in my absence, work out your salvation with fear and trembling, for it is God who is at work in you, both to will and to work for His good pleasure" (Philippians 2:12-13). We see clearly through the life of Paul that courage doesn't necessarily mean you're not afraid. Most often bravery is actually demonstrated in the face of fear. It is only in facing our fears that they can be conquered and our destiny captured.

It is only in facing our fears that they can be conquered and our destiny captured.

Many people are under the illusion that brave people are somehow immune to anxiety. This is simply not true. Fear is a human emotion common to everyone. Luke describes Jesus' emotional state hours before He was crucified. He said Jesus was in agony to the point where He was sweating drops of blood (see Luke 22:44). I would say this was a manifestation of pretty intense fear. Courage is not an emotional state, but rather the choice we make to overcome our feelings so that we can obtain our desired outcome.

Type-Two Courage

There is another kind of courage that is also demonstrated throughout the Bible. I am talking about unreasonable, supernatural courage that transcends the mind, will and emotions. Acts 4 and 5 give us a perfect example of supernatural courage:

And when they had summoned them, they commanded them not to speak or teach at all in the name of Jesus. But Peter and John answered and said to them, "Whether it is right in the sight of God to give heed to you rather than to God, you be the judge; for we cannot stop speaking about what we have seen and heard." When they had threatened them further, they let them go (finding no basis on which to punish them). . . . When they had been released, they went to their own companions and reported all that the chief priests and the elders had said to them. And when they heard this, they lifted their voices to God with one accord and said, "O Lord, it is You who MADE THE HEAVEN AND THE EARTH AND THE SEA, AND ALL THAT IS IN THEM, who by the Holy Spirit, through the mouth of our father David Your servant, said, 'WHY DID THE GENTILES RAGE, AND THE PEOPLES DEVISE FUTILE THINGS? THE KINGS OF THE EARTH TOOK THEIR STAND, AND THE RULERS WERE GATHERED TOGETHER AGAINST THE LORD AND AGAINST HIS CHRIST.' For truly in this city there were gathered together against Your holy servant Jesus, whom You anointed, both Herod and Pontius Pilate, along with the Gentiles and the peoples of Israel, to do whatever Your hand and Your purpose predestined to occur. And now, Lord, take note of their threats, and grant that *Your bond-servants may speak Your word with all confidence,* while You extend Your hand to heal, and signs and wonders take place through the name of Your holy servant Jesus." And when they had prayed, the place where they had gathered together was shaken, and they were all filled with the Holy Spirit and began to speak the word of God with boldness (Acts 4:18-21,23-31, emphasis added).

And after calling the apostles in, they flogged them and ordered them not to speak in the name of Jesus, and then released them. So they went on their way from the presence of the Council, rejoicing that they had been considered worthy to suffer shame for His name. And every day, in the temple and from house to house, they kept right on teaching and preaching Jesus as the Christ (Acts 5:40-42).

We can't psych ourselves up into supernatural courage. It is a divine boldness that can only be imparted by the Lord Himself. When we receive this gift of courage, we feel as though there is an invisible force field protecting us.

My Story

I've experienced this kind of courage on many occasions in my life. One of the more dramatic of these occurred in the summer of 1994. Kathy and I took our son's eighth-grade class, consisting of eight kids, to Santa Cruz beach to celebrate their graduation. We headed for home at dusk in a borrowed 15-passenger van. A couple hours into our homeward journey, the kids wanted to stop so they could go to the restroom. We pulled off the freeway and stopped at a convenience store. The kids piled out, went to the bathroom, grabbed something to eat, and piled back in. As we entered the freeway onramp, I noticed in my rearview mirror an old white Chevy pickup truck tailgating us. I probably wouldn't have thought much about it except I heard a voice in my spirit say, "Peace be with you. No harm shall come to any of you." *What a strange thing to hear,* I thought, but an intense, overwhelming peace came over me. It felt like I had jumped into an ocean of courage.

After we entered the freeway, the tailgating truck pulled alongside us. The driver rolled down his passenger window and started shouting and motioning to me to pull over. I slowed the van and began to exit onto the shoulder of the road, still trying to interpret the man's concerns. By now, his yelling and motioning had grown more intense. I lowered my window and further reduced my speed as he pulled within inches of the van. I thought I could hear him say that our rear tire was flat, so I came to a stop and the Chevy truck stopped right next to us. He seemed oblivious to the fact that his truck was blocking one lane of the freeway. He continued yelling something, but I couldn't understand a word he was saying. Then something crazy happened: I looked into his eyes and they were *glowing red*! I don't mean he had pinkeye or he looked tired—I mean his eyes were *glowing*. Then I heard a small voice inside me say, *Get out of here!*

I shouted, "Thank you," to the man and began to maneuver my way back onto the freeway. As I did, the man's mood turned to rage and he ran us off the road, boxing us in against the freeway fence. Then he jumped out of the truck—I now saw that he was a white man in his early thirties, wearing a ragged T-shirt and dirty jeans—and began to run for the passenger door of the van. One of the kids screamed, "He has a gun!"

I threw the van into drive and floored it, narrowly squeezing between the fence and his truck. As I cleared the Chevy, I glanced into my rearview mirror and saw the guy running for his vehicle. I stepped on it, hoping to lose him quickly and exit the freeway. But within seconds he was right on our tail, trying to ram us from behind. The kids started freaking out, yelling, "He's going to ram us! He's trying to hit us from behind!" I smashed the accelerator to the floor and our speed increased to 80, then 90, then 100 miles per hour. But the old truck stayed within inches of our bumper.

Meanwhile, fear had overwhelmed the van. Kathy and the kids were shouting and crying. One eighth-grade boy unbuckled his seat belt and jumped up in the van, yelling, "We are all going to die! We are going to die!" He grabbed the side-door handle and tried to open it, apparently planning to leap out of the vehicle. My son, Jason, and his friend, Andy, quickly unstrapped themselves and wrestled him to the floor, restraining him as he continued to freak out.

Kathy became hysterical and began pleading with me to pull over. But an amazing peace kept washing over me like warm water. The peace was so intense that I found myself laughing through much of the ordeal. I don't think anyone else saw the humor in it at all, especially my wife!

The crazy guy continued to try to slam into us as I veered from lane to lane, using the entire freeway to avoid a collision. The other cars on the road began to slow down and give us room to maneuver as they observed the assault.

I couldn't lose him, so about 40 miles into the chase I decided to pull over and see what he would do with so many witnesses watching him. I came to a complete stop on the right shoulder of the road. Traffic in both directions came to a halt. To my surprise, he pulled into the median and turned his truck sideways. Then he headed right for us at full speed and tried to crash into us from the side. I stepped on the gas, narrowly escaping his attack. He crashed into the freeway fence and his truck got stuck in the deep gravel shoulder.

I jumped on the accelerator, and the large van roared to speeds of over 110 miles per hour. Cars on the road pulled over to let us through as we tried to race to safety. Several minutes passed, and then suddenly, as if from nowhere, the white Chevy truck appeared in my rearview mirror again. Within seconds he managed to get alongside us. I swerved back and forth over the entire road, even using the gravel shoulders on both sides of the freeway to escape his assault. Several times, I sped up to 100 miles per hour and then slammed on the brakes, swerving just as he was about to ram us from behind and forcing him to pass us. Then I would drive hard to stay behind him.

Finally, we passed a highway patrolman who had someone pulled over on the right shoulder of the road. I slammed on the brakes and pulled into the median. The madman pulled in front of me and tried to sideswipe me as he skidded to a stop. I jammed it into reverse and floored it, desperately trying to get back near the patrol car.

At last the officer came into our sights. Kathy rolled down her window and began shouting hysterically to the officer, "He is trying to kill us! Please help us! He is trying to kill us!"

I came to a stop in the median. There were just three lanes separating us from the officer. I tried to wait there as Kathy continued struggling to get the cop's attention. It was starting to get dark by now and I knew the crazy guy was near, but I couldn't figure out where he had stopped.

All of a sudden, the back door of the van opened and the girls in the back seat starting screaming, "He has gotten in the back door! He is getting in the van!" Reaching over the seat, the girls managed to hold the door partway closed.

"Hold on!" I shouted.

I forced the shifter into drive and jumped on it, throwing the man to the ground. I wanted to stay close to the patrolman, so I stopped once more, hoping he would see us. But the nutcase who was chasing us jumped up on the running boards, forced the window open and managed to unlock the side door. Jason and Andy were still restraining the boy on the floor as he continued screaming and trying to escape. Jason reached up with one hand, grasped the door handle and struggled to hold the door closed, yelling, "Dad, he is getting in the side door!"

"Hang on!" I shouted back. I dropped it in reverse and floored the accelerator. Again the perpetrator fell off the van. I began speeding forward and backward to keep him out of the van, still trying to remain in the view of the officer.

All at once, I heard someone outside the van yell, "Stop, or I will blow your f—ing head off!" *Good*, I thought, *the cops finally got him.* But when I turned and looked ahead, I saw that the highway patrolman had his gun pointed right at my head, just inches from the windshield.

"Out of the van!" he commanded. I slowly unbuckled my seatbelt and opened the door. He put his gun in my chest and threw me to the ground. I pleaded with him, "You have got the wrong guy. Dude, you are arresting the wrong man!" He cuffed me from behind and dragged me to the passenger's side of the van. I saw then that the crazy guy was lying on the ground in handcuffs also. Within seconds, highway patrol cars, police cars and a helicopter encircled us.

Even in cuffs, incredible peace continued to flow over me. I over-heard the crazy guy telling the police that I had kidnapped his daughter. The officers lined our girls up against the van and asked him to identify his daughter. When he couldn't find her, they hauled him off in the patrol car. When the story was finally straight, they released me, and we drove home without further incident.

At six o'clock the next morning, the phone rang. Startled and groggy, I picked it up. "Hello," I grunted. There was a long pause, but I could hear someone quietly weeping on the other end. "Hello," I said, a little more cheerfully this time.

"Hi, I am officer Jones, the man who arrested you last night." Choking back tears, he continued, "I wanted to apologize to you for treating you that way." Unable to disguise his weeping, he went on, "When your wife said, 'He is trying to kill us,' and the man said you kidnapped his daughter, I thought you were the assailant. When you wouldn't stop the van, I decided to shoot you to save the family. But as I aimed my gun and squeezed the trigger, something said, 'Don't shoot!' I have been on the force for 20 years and have never pulled my gun on anyone. I almost killed you!"

"Oh don't worry about it," I answered. "I am a Christian and the Lord told me when it all started, 'Peace be with you and no harm shall come to anyone.' So you couldn't have shot me." Apparently shocked, and still crying, the officer hung up. If we are going to transform cities, disciple nations and see heaven literally come to earth, it is going to take true valor: supernatural courage that defies the intelligent, confronts the political spirit and forces the dogs of doom to back down. Most of the eighth-grade class was so powerfully moved by God's divine protection that each of them got up in front of the church on Sunday morning and shared how much the trip had impacted them. (The boy that was held down on the floor of the van was pretty traumatized. He had to see a counselor for about a year before he finally got past it. Kathy also dealt with some fear for quite a while.) The story of God's supernatural protection circulated through our small town for many years.

It is time for us to ask heaven for an infusion of boldness that possesses our souls and inspires our spirits!

Notes

1. Malcolm Gladwell, *The Tipping Point: How Little Things Can Make a Big Difference* (New York: Back Bay Books, 2002), p. 28.
2. Quotes from "Things That Will Never Happen," Rense.com. http://www.rense.com/general81/dw.htm.
3. John Lennon, "Imagine," from the album *Imagine*. © 1971 Apple Records.
4. Mick Jagger and Keith Richards, "(I Can't Get No) Satisfaction," from the album *Out of Our Heads*. © 1965 London Records.

5

Living in the Land of the Giants

Excellence is the result of caring more than
others think is wise, risking more than others think is safe,
dreaming more than others think is practical,
and expecting more than others think is possible.
AUTHOR UNKNOWN

Tall Poppies

It was a warm summer afternoon in Australia. About 200 leaders had gathered for a leadership conference where I was teaching on the subject of greatness. I wanted to use some examples that my audience could relate to in order to emphasize the fact that it is heroes who make history. However, I was unfamiliar with Australia's past, so I asked the crowd, "Who are the heroes in your nation?" They were completely silent. After a few moments of increasing tension, I pressed, "Come on, Aussies, who are the most famous people in Australia? You know what I mean. The U.S. has George Washington, Abraham Lincoln and Billy Graham. England has Winston Churchill, and South Africa has Nelson Mandela. Who are the heroes of this country?"

The hush continued in the room. Finally, the senior leader on the front row broke the silence. "Kris," he whispered, obviously trying not to embarrass me. "We don't have heroes in our nation. It's culturally taboo to be great in Australia. It's called the Tall Poppy Syndrome."

After the meeting ended, some of the pastoral team came over and explained to me that the tall poppy syndrome is a social dynamic in which anyone who accomplishes something outstanding or somehow stands above the crowd is cut down by the masses. I was stunned to learn this was a guiding principle in their culture, and wondered if they understood that this societal dynamic inherently leads people to resist advancement, innovation or progress. As I pondered the Australian mindset, however, it occurred to me that much of the Body of Christ has the identical culture. Plenty of churches are teaching people how to be *good*, but few are inspiring people to *greatness*.

Plenty of churches are teaching
people how to be *good*, but few are
inspiring people to *greatness*.

Humility and Greatness

False humility is largely to blame for the Church's tall poppy syndrome. In my first book, *The Supernatural Ways of Royalty*, I investigated the true nature of humility. At the risk of being redundant, I want to briefly review one biblical example that demonstrates how true humility is entirely compatible with confidence, strength and every other aspect of greatness.

The fourth chapter of Daniel records the testimony of King Nebuchadnezzar, who had a dream about a huge tree that covered the earth and became shade for the animals, birds and creatures of the planet. In the midst of this amazing vision, the king heard a voice shout:

> Chop down the tree and cut off its branches, strip off its foliage and scatter its fruit; let the beasts flee from under it and the birds from its branches. Yet leave the stump with its roots in the ground, but with a band of iron and bronze around it in the new grass of the field; and let him be drenched with the dew of heaven, and let him share with the beasts in the grass of the earth. Let his mind be changed from that of a man and let a beast's mind be given to him, and let seven periods of time pass over him (Daniel 4:14-16).

The king was understandably freaked out by the dream and called in his top spiritual consultants to interpret it. Just as the magicians, conjurers and diviners were telling the king that they couldn't translate the dream, Daniel walked into the room. (You've got to love this guy's timing; he always seemed to be just a little late everywhere he went.) Nebuchadnezzar related the dream to Daniel, who immediately got the interpretation from God.

What Daniel did next may be a little off the subject of humility, but it is still worth commenting on. Before he explained the meaning of the dream, Daniel said to the king, "My lord, if only the dream applied to those who hate you and its interpretation to your adversaries!" (Daniel 4:19). Daniel truly loved the kings he served in spite of the fact that they destroyed his country, probably killed his family and took him captive to serve at their will. Nebuchadnezzar was so wicked. But there is a powerful lesson embedded in this story. If we are ever going to be invited into the palace to advise kings and mentor nations, we had better figure out how to love our enemies and help leaders we don't agree with.

Now back to the story. Daniel explained that the tree the angel chopped down in the dream actually represented Nebuchadnezzar! Apparently, the king's destructive behavior, arrogance and pride had finally gotten him in hot water with God, and the Lord of heaven was about to discipline him severely. Daniel went on to counsel Nebuchadnezzar to try to avoid this calamity by humbling himself. But the hardheaded king didn't listen, and a year later, his world came crashing in on him. Here is the account of his demise:

> Twelve months later he was walking on the roof of the royal palace of Babylon. The king reflected and said, "Is this not Babylon the great, which I myself have built as a royal residence by the might of my power and for the glory of my majesty?" While the word was in the king's mouth, a voice came from heaven, saying, "King Nebuchadnezzar, to you it is declared: sovereignty has been removed from you, and you will be driven away from mankind, and your dwelling place will be with the beasts of the field. You will be given grass to eat like cattle, and seven periods of time will pass over you until you recognize that the Most High is ruler over the realm of mankind and bestows it on whomever He wishes." Immediately the word concerning Nebuchadnezzar was fulfilled; and he was driven away from mankind and began eating grass like cattle, and his body was drenched with the dew of heaven until his hair had grown like eagles' feathers and his nails like birds' claws (Daniel 4:29-33).

The insane king lived in exile for seven years. Finally, that terrible season came to an end, and God restored him. Evidently, Nebuchadnezzar kept a journal of his restoration, as his thoughts and reflections became part of the book of Daniel. King Nebuchadnezzar wrote:

> At that time my reason returned to me. And my majesty and splendor were restored to me for the glory of my kingdom, and my counselors and my nobles began seeking me out; so I was reestablished in my sovereignty, and surpassing greatness was added to me. Now I, Nebuchadnezzar, praise, exalt and honor the King of heaven, for all His works are true and His ways just, and He is able to humble those who walk in pride (Daniel 4:36-37).

The truth of God's grace humbles a man without degrading him, and exalts a man without inflating him!

God removed the king because of his arrogance and self-absorbed lifestyle. But when the Almighty restored Nebuchadnezzar's mind, the king said *humbly* that he had *majesty, splendor, glory, sovereignty and surpassing greatness!* The obvious point here is that humility isn't feeling bad about yourself or thinking you are little, insignificant or anything else demeaning. True humility begins with remembering the source of your greatness. The truth of God's grace humbles a man without degrading him, and exalts a man without inflating him!

Being Exalted

Humility is not only compatible with greatness; it is the process of significance. We see this clearly in Jesus' statement:

"Whoever exalts himself shall be humbled; and whoever humbles himself shall be exalted" (Matthew 23:12). According to Christ, the act of humility is the pathway to promotion. Jesus was not criticizing the desire for greatness; He was *encouraging* it by showing us how to attain it!

So often in the Church we have emphasized the process while demeaning the promise.

Hopefully, we all agree that Jesus is the model of humility, as He is of all other things. If this is true, then we only need to ask ourselves one simple question: What happened when Jesus humbled Himself? Paul tells us:

> [Jesus] emptied Himself, taking the form of a bond-servant, and being made in the likeness of men. . . . For this reason also, *God highly exalted Him*, and bestowed on Him the name which is above every name, so that at the name of Jesus EVERY KNEE WILL BOW, of those who are in heaven and on earth and under the earth, and that every tongue will confess that Jesus Christ is Lord, to the glory of God the Father (Philippians 2:7, 9-11, emphasis added).

Just in case you were wondering, being exalted means being *raised high*. In the Kingdom, humility is designed to make us tall poppies! Yet, so often in the Church we have emphasized the process while demeaning the promise, which in turn creates frustration and confusion. We must remove this contradiction from our core values and begin to allow those who submit to the process that Jesus modeled to receive its intended reward.

A House of Heroes

I can't help but notice that all 12 men who hung out with Jesus, though they came from different occupations and backgrounds, eventually had one thing in common. They all thought they were supposed to be great. There's something about the presence of Jesus that causes people to dream of prominence, grandeur and greatness. If we are going to see a reformation in the Church that translates into true global transformation, we are going to have to cultivate, encourage and embrace a house of heroes.

The book of Nehemiah tells us that Jerusalem had a house of mighty men. The book of Nehemiah can be read as a "type" of the restoring work of the Holy Spirit (the Comforter—Nehemiah means "God comforts"); and each element of Jerusalem's restoration points to the things the Holy Spirit is rebuilding in the Church. It was King David who originally established the "house of the mighty men" (Nehemiah 3:16). Like Jesus after him, David had a way of turning weaklings into warriors. (Can you imagine a house where the mighty men of David lived together? Now that's what I call neighborhood watch.) David's mighty men lived together in the same "house," which allowed them to establish and sustain a heroic culture. You can bet there was no such thing as the Tall Poppy Syndrome in David's house of heroes!

Noble Men

If the Church is going to become a place where mighty men and women can be trained, equipped and deployed, then we need leaders who are like Jesus and David. As I discussed in *The Supernatural Ways of Royalty,* the primary reason false humility persists in the Church is that we still don't really know who we are in God. We need confident fathers to be restored to the Body of Christ to reestablish the royal identity of the people of God. Jesus' supreme confidence in His identity as the Son of God enabled Him to call out sonship in His disciples. David's kingly identity, which he embraced long before he ever sat on a throne, caused him to turn a band of rejects into a company of royal warriors. If we are going to develop a culture that deploys world changers, leaders must first be established in their own identity in God. We need Jesus to hang out with us in such a way that we become possessed by the same sense of royal identity and epic vision that His disciples experienced in the days when He walked this planet.

Absent or Empowering

There are lots of leaders who think they are empowering their people but are actually just absent. Empowering others and being absent from them are not the same thing! A father who rarely comes home would never be mistaken for being an empowering presence in his household. A leader who hardly ever comes out of his office or seldom interacts with his team is like a father who never comes home. He may think that he is being empowering by removing the negative element of control from the culture. But people don't necessarily feel powerful just because nobody is resisting them. More often than not, their leader's absence leaves them feeling lost, abandoned and unsure of what they are supposed to be doing. Empowering leaders have a proactive, not inactive, ability. They do not simply remove the controlling dynamics; they establish positive elements of communication, encouragement, direction, praise and cooperation.

Incidentally, absent leaders can be just as controlling as the ones who get into everybody's business. We most often think of controlling leaders as micromanagers or angry people who rule through fear and intimidation. Actually, one of the most common ways to control people is to withdraw and withhold information. Jesus put it this way: "No longer do I call you slaves, for the slave does not know what his master is doing; but I have called you friends, for all things that I have heard from My Father I have made known to you" (John 15:15). Jesus equated withholding information with slavery.

Empowering others and being absent from them are not the same thing!

A great example of how withholding information enslaves people is found in the Genesis story of Joseph. Joseph interpreted Pharaoh's dreams as being about seven years of plenty followed by seven years of famine. Then he wisely instructed Pharaoh to store 20 percent of all the grain in Egypt in the seven years of abundance so there would be enough food to feed the nation in the famine (see Genesis 41). But Joseph withheld the revelation about the coming famine and the plan to store food from the Egyptian population. The result was that all of the Egyptian inhabitants became slaves as they sold themselves to Pharaoh for food!

> "Why should we die before your eyes, both we and our land? Buy us and our land for food, and we and our land will be slaves to Pharaoh. So give us seed, that we may live and not die, and that the land may not be desolate."

So Joseph bought all the land of Egypt for Pharaoh, for every Egyptian sold his field, because the famine was severe upon them. Thus the land became Pharaoh's (Genesis 47:19-20).

If Joseph had simply shared with the people the same revelation he gave to Pharaoh, the Egyptians would have become the richest people on the planet, because the famine affected the entire known world and people came from every nation to purchase food. Instead, Joseph's secret created a two-class system (rich and poor), and a first-world nation became a third-world nation in one generation. Symptomatic cures, however, become tomorrow's problems. The next pharaoh who rose to power enslaved the Israelites (see Exodus 1). Incidentally, it is important to understand what kind of ecosystem our decisions create for future generations!

Empowering leaders make decisions *with* people, not just *for* people.

Empowering leaders make decisions *with* people, not just *for* people. When we withhold information from our people or tell them just what they need to know to get their job done, we produce slave camps in which one person does all the thinking. This is religion on steroids. Religion wants to tame people, to domesticate the masses and get them to keep the rules. But new ideas are never discovered behind the iron bars of the zoo. It's only in the uncharted jungle of life that new realities and opportunities are revealed. If we are going to become a house of heroes, we need fresh ideas, untried solutions, innovation and bold, courageous thoughts delivered by risk takers, not zookeepers.

Religion wants to tame people,
to domesticate the masses and
get them to keep the rules. New ideas
are never discovered behind
the iron bars of the zoo.

In His friendship with His disciples, Jesus did not merely tell them *what* to think; He taught them *how* to think through conversations and interactions. He didn't keep them on the sidelines, watching Him do everything. They had permission to ask questions, to try to do what He was doing and to get feedback from Him. More than that, Jesus told them to do even greater things than He did! True Kingdom-minded fathers and mothers want their sons and daughters to succeed them and exceed them.

Living for the Reward

We will never nurture greatness in people without cultivating a culture of reward. I would like to propose to you that no truly great feat has ever been accomplished without (at least in part) the promise of reward. For example, David killed Goliath so that he could marry the king's daughter (see 1 Samuel 17:25). The Israelites left Egypt to obtain a Promised Land (see Exodus 3:8,17). Jesus Himself achieved His greatest victory for the sake of reward: "For the joy set before Him He endured the cross" (Hebrews 12:2). History books are full of stories of godly people who accomplished great things *for the sake of reward.*

We will never nurture greatness in people without cultivating a culture of reward.

But reward has become a dirty word in many religious circles. Some have deemed it unspiritual even to think of rewarding people for their efforts. If you were a carpenter, mechanic or any other occupation, for that matter, it would never dawn on you to do your job and have your employer decide how much to pay you after you are done with the work. Yet, if you are a conference speaker in some Christian circles, you had better not act like you even care about how much the offering is. If you require a certain dollar amount per session when you speak at conferences, you will most likely be tagged as a materialist. Don't worry, I never ask for an offering when I speak, and I am well taken care of.

Neither am I advocating that we should work for money instead of working for God. But I am saying that God intends for us to be motivated by reward in working for Him as surely as our employers do. The fact that we struggle over things like paying spiritual leaders a wage for their labors indicates that we don't truly understand God's heavenly economy. It is spiritual to expect God to compensate us for our efforts. Jesus said, "The laborer is worthy of his wages" (Luke 10:7). The last chapter of the Good Book says, "Behold, I am coming quickly, and My *reward* is with Me, to render to every man according to what he has done" (Revelation 22:12, emphasis added). The parables of the ten talents, the ten minas and the sower are all about working for a reward.

Reward is the driving motivation of our *faith*. The writer of Hebrews says, "Without faith it is impossible to please Him, for he who comes to God must believe that He is and that He is a rewarder of those who seek Him" (Hebrews 11:6, emphasis added). When people argue that Christians shouldn't care about reward, it is like saying you shouldn't believe in God. You simply can't please God unless you expect Him to reward you.

One of the main ways we create a culture of reward is by celebrating people's accomplishments. Thus, it is no surprise that folks who struggle with the idea of reward also resist compliments, praise or acknowledgment of their achievements. I have been to churches where they don't even clap when the worship band rocks. In some circles, celebrating people's efforts is seen as unspiritual, self-promoting or arrogant. Many people actually believe that recognizing a person's success steals glory from God. But isn't it God who created us and gave each of us special gifts and abilities? We cheer for our kids when they are playing sports. We never think, "They are stealing my glory." Actually, when one of my kids does something amazing on the court or field, I turn to the other parents and say, "Whose kid is that?" Everyone laughs and says, "We know, it's yours!"

**When we imitate God,
we are being ourselves.**

The truth is that when we do something awesome on the earth, God is the loudest one in the stands of life, cheering us on, saying things like, "*Whose* son is that? That kid takes after his Daddy! That girl is amazing!" The great exploits of God's sons and daughters actually glorify the Father! That's why Paul wrote, "Be imitators of God, as beloved children" (Ephesians 5:1). When we imitate God, we are being ourselves. We were created in His image and are commanded to become Christlike. Therefore, there is nothing too noble to reach for, too awesome to believe for, too powerful to hope for or too excellent to live for . . . because we are children of the *King!*

Serial Killers

Jealousy is the evil adversary of greatness. It begins as a selfish sin, but like a watchman who deliberately dislodges the royal gates, allowing a vicious enemy access, jealousy is a serial killer! The apostle James warns us that what is initiated as a struggle in our hearts eventually gives place to demonic spirits that wreak havoc on the very core of our being:

> But if you have bitter jealousy and selfish ambition in your heart, do not be arrogant and so lie against the truth. This wisdom is not that which comes down from above, but is *earthly, natural, demonic. For where jealousy and selfish ambition exist,* there is disorder and *every evil thing* (James 3:14-16, emphasis added).

The account of Saul and David returning from the most famous battle in Jewish history illustrates this point so well:

> It happened as they were coming, when David returned from killing the Philistine, that the women came out of all the cities of Israel, singing and dancing, to meet King Saul, with tambourines, with joy and with musical instruments. The women sang as they played, and said, "Saul has slain his thousands, and David his ten

thousands." Then Saul became very angry, for this saying displeased him; and he said, "They have ascribed to David ten thousands, but to me they have ascribed thousands. Now what more can he have but the kingdom?" *Saul looked at David with suspicion [jealousy] from that day on.* Now it came about on the next day that *an evil spirit from God came mightily upon Saul,* and he raved in the midst of the house, while David was playing the harp with his hand, as usual; and a spear was in Saul's hand. Saul hurled the spear for he thought, "I will pin David to the wall." But David escaped from his presence twice. Now Saul was afraid of David, for the LORD was with him but had departed from Saul (1 Samuel 18:6-12, emphasis added).

David was Saul's spiritual son, and he had just killed Goliath, eliminating the greatest threat in Israel's history. It was the presence of giants that kept more than a million people out of the land of God's promises. But instead of King Saul behaving like a father and celebrating his son's victory, he became jealous and suspicious of David. This created an axis of evil in the interior of his soul, attracting evil spirits of insanity and murder that tormented Saul into trying to destroy David.

This pattern is repeated over and over all throughout the Bible. For instance, there was Cain, who murdered his brother Abel because he was jealous of Abel's relationship with God (see Genesis 4). There was Joseph the dreamer, whose brothers hated him because of his grand vision and his father's favor. Their jealousy ultimately drove them to sell Joseph into slavery (see Genesis 37). And who can forget Jesus' disciples, whose envy toward one another kept them in a perpetual state of competition (see Mark 10:35-41; Luke 9:46)?

The tall poppy syndrome is the fruit of leaders who react to these sibling rivalries by changing the structure to eliminate jealousy instead of dealing with the heart issues. It is interesting to note that Jesus cultivated a culture that potentially fostered jealousy by favoring a few disciples. For example, He took only Peter, James and John with Him to the Mount of Transfiguration (see Mark 9:1-4). When He raised the synagogue official's daughter from the dead, He put everyone out of the room except the same three guys (see Mark 5:37). When Jesus was stressed out before the crucifixion, He only invited Peter, James and John to pray with Him in the Garden of Gethsemane. Although *all* the disciples fought amongst themselves for prominence, Jesus did nothing to dispel their envy of one another, but continued to favor the same three guys. In other words, Jesus refused to change their circumstances to deal with their character issues. His prescription for their jealousy was simple: humble yourselves by becoming like a child (see Matthew 18:1-4).

We need to understand that our circumstances never *cause* heart issues; they only reveal them.

We need to understand that our circumstances never *cause* heart issues; they only reveal them. When leaders adjust the conditions of people's circumstances to accommodate their sins, they become peacekeepers (not to be confused with peacemakers) who choose to silence people's complaining instead of allowing the crucible of their state of affairs to purify their hearts. But in a dark corner of the silent sanctuary wall of the soul creeps the poisonous mold of evil. This often goes completely unnoticed until one day the heart is attacked, causing irreversible damage or even death. Therefore, whenever we let sin (jealousy is sin) dictate our choices, we have already reduced the impact of our movement down to the loudest voice of immaturity in the room. This attitude ultimately derails our God-given destiny.

> Whenever we let sin (jealousy is sin)
> dictate our choices, we have already
> reduced the impact of our movement
> down to the loudest voice of
> immaturity in the room.

Pastor Cleddie Keith says, "If you're jealous of someone, invest in them, and then their victory will be your victory." It is paramount that leaders create a culture of reward in which sons and daughters recognize that victories are always a family affair, creating a kind of synergistic amplification that eventually benefits everyone.

Who Will Follow the Heart of the King?

Celebrating instead of competing with the victories of others creates a "team first" mentality. Teamwork is the result of everyone taking ownership of the corporate mission. John Maxwell, who has written many books on leadership, once said, "People support what they help create." The goal of every great leader must be to transfer ownership of the mission to his team, flock or staff. When people take ownership of the corporate call, they need very little oversight, because their souls are possessed by the heart of the King.

This principle is so powerfully captured in the story of King Robert the Bruce and his courageous soldiers. Although the movie *Braveheart* depicts William Wallace as the hero of Scotland, the real hero was Robert the Bruce. Wallace won many battles against the English, but it was King Robert who finally freed his nation from the tyranny of the British. Historian Henrietta (H. E.) Marshall tells the story this way:

> King Robert did not live long to enjoy the peace which at last had come to the land. He was not an old man, but he had lived such a hard life that he seemed older than he was. Now he became so ill that he knew he could not live long.
>
> When he felt that he was dying, he called all his nobles and wise men to him. As they stood round him, Bruce told them that he must soon die, and bade them honour his little son David as their King.
>
> With tears of sorrow the nobles promised to do as the King asked.
>
> Bruce then turned to the good Lord James. "My dearest and best friend," he said, "you know how hard I have had to fight for my kingdom. At the time when I was sorest pressed, I made a vow that when God should grant me peace, I should go to the Holy Land to fight for the Sepulchre of Christ. But now that I have peace, my body is feeble, and I cannot fulfil my heart's desire. Yet I would fain send my heart whither my body cannot go. There is no knight so gallant as you, my dear and special friend. Therefore I pray you, when I am dead take my heart from my body, carry it to the Holy Land, and there bury it."

At first Douglas could not speak for tears. After a few minutes he said, "Gallant and noble King, I thank you a thousand times for the honour you do me. Your command shall be obeyed."

"Dear friend, I thank you. You give me your promise?" said the Bruce.

"Most willingly. Upon my knighthood I swear it."

"Thanks be to God. Now I die in peace, since I know that the bravest knight in all my kingdom will do for me what I cannot do for myself," said the King, as he lay back content.

Not many days after this the great King died. From all the land there arose a cry of mourning and sorrow. With tears and sobs, with the sound of sad music and wailing, the people followed their King to his last resting place in Dunfermline Abbey. . . .

Wrapped in a robe of cloth of gold the great King was laid to rest, and a beautiful tomb of white marble was raised over his grave. Long ago the tomb has disappeared, but the place where Robert the Bruce lies is still pointed out in the Abbey of Dunfermline.

True to his promise, the Douglas ordered the heart of Bruce to be taken from his body after he was dead. The heart was then embalmed. That is, it was prepared with sweet-smelling spices and other things to keep it from decay. Douglas enclosed the heart in a beautiful box of silver and enamel, which he hung round his neck by a chain of silk and gold. Then, with a noble company of knights and squires, he set sail for Palestine.

On his way he passed through Spain. There he heard that the King of Spain was fighting against the Saracens. The Saracens were the people who had possession of

Palestine. They were unkind to the Christians, and insulted their religion. Douglas therefore thought that he would be doing right to help the King of Spain, before passing on to the Holy Land.

The armies met, and there was a great battle. The Scots charged so furiously that the Saracens fled before them. But thinking that the Spaniards were following to help them, the Scots chased the fleeing foe too far. Too late, Douglas found that he and his little band were cut off from their friends, and entirely surrounded by the fierce, dark faces of the enemy.

There was no escape. All that was left to do was to die fighting. Taking the silver box containing King Robert's heart from his neck, Douglas threw it into the thickest of the fight, crying, "On, gallant heart, as thou wert ever wont, the Douglas will follow thee or die." Then springing after it, he fiercely fought until he fell, pierced with many wounds. Round him fell most of the brave company of nobles who had set sail with him.

When the battle was over, the few who remained sought for their leader. They found him lying dead above the heart of Bruce.[1]

When we lay our life down for the heart of the King, we capture His passion and find our divine purpose. True greatness is only found as we die to selfish ambition, jealousy, envy and strife and embrace a noble culture that protects the heart of the King.

Note
  1. Henrietta Elizabeth Marshall, *Scotland's Story: A History of Scotland for Boys and Girls* (London: Thomas Nelson and Sons Ltd., 1907), pp. 185-187.

6

Iron Sharpens Iron

Nearly all men can stand adversity,
but if you want to test a man's character, give him power.
ABRAHAM LINCOLN

An Empowering Culture
Confronts People

If we are going to see famous people emerge from the Body of Christ, then it is imperative that we develop an empowering culture. But we must realize that empowering people means giving their latent tendencies, whether good, bad or ugly, opportunities to grow and find expression. And unless we have ways of confronting the bad and the ugly when they are exposed, we will make room for a kind of spiritual cancer in the Body. Cancer cells are the fastest-growing cells in a body, but they live a self-absorbed existence, growing at the expense of everything else. They ultimately destroy the very thing that gave them life. Similarly, people who allow selfish ambition to dictate their own agendas instead of living to benefit the whole family become a cancer to the Body of Christ.

It is important to understand that certain cultural elements actually facilitate and encourage this sick social and spiritual dynamic. I experienced this firsthand many years ago when I was asked to help resolve a conflict between two leaders. One leader was a young man who spent many years serving his senior leader in a vibrant church, with the promise of being his successor at a specified time. When the date came and went without any sign of passing the baton, the younger leader began to get restless. After several conversations in which the senior leader felt like he was being "pushed out," it became apparent that he had changed his mind and decided not to step aside. In time, the associate pastor asked to be sent out to plant his own church. The leader agreed, threw a going-away party for him, took an offering for the new work and publicly encouraged his congregants to go with him.

But a few months later, the senior pastor found out that I was helping this brother start his church, and he was livid! He called me and wanted to know what I was doing supporting a church split! When I recounted the facts to him, as I understood them, he acknowledged that the story was accurate, but said that his former associate pastor (whom he had mentored for nearly two decades) was "an Absalom" (see 2 Samuel 14:25). When I hung up the phone, I was so confused. This senior leader took an offering for the younger leader, publicly prayed for him, and so on, but after he left, decided he was an Absalom. I was supposed to talk to these leaders again the next day, so I decided to ask the Lord what to do.

It takes a David to create an Absalom!

Immediately the Lord said, "It takes a David to create an Absalom!" Wow! I was stunned. David was a man after God's own heart (see Acts 13:22). "How could David help create an Absalom?" I enquired. The Lord directed me to examine the books of Samuel in order to understand this unhealthy leadership dynamic.

A Dysfunctional Leader
After God's Heart

David had six sons born to him from six different wives (see 2 Samuel 3:2-5). David's wife Ahinoam was mother to Amnon, who was David's oldest son. Amnon fell in love with Absalom's sister, Tamar, the daughter of Maacah, another of David's wives. When Amnon became aggressive in his pursuit of Tamar, she sent him packing. But he became so obsessed with her beauty that he violently raped her (see 2 Samuel 13:1-19).

When word came to King David about his daughter's rape, he was incensed, but he didn't do a darn thing about it, which turned out to be a pattern throughout his life. When Absalom, Tamar's brother, found out about it, he took her into his home, where she stayed until the day she died. Absalom's name means "my father is my peace," and like his name suggests, he was a peacemaker, the kind of person who needs someone to bring justice to wrongs so there can be peace. As each day passed without any closure, Absalom's anger grew until he secretly devised a plot to kill Amnon.

After having Amnon murdered, Absalom fled the country to save his own life. He lived in exile for a number of years, yet longed for his father. Through a series of complex circumstances, he managed to get back into his dad's palace. But though Amnon was dead, Absalom never forgave his father for not confronting him about Tamar's rape. Bitterness escalated in him until it possessed his soul. Revenge drove him to stand at the entrance of his father's courtroom for four years telling people they would not get justice in that court until he was king (see 2 Samuel 15:7, *NIV*).

Eventually, Absalom convinced the Israelites that he was the righteous leader who would bring them justice. Ultimately, Absalom's self-promoting tactics won him the heart of the nation.

Can you imagine one of your kids undermining you for four years in your own house and your never saying anything to him? I mean, not even a little, "Hey, Ab, I heard you might have a . . . like . . . uh . . . slight disagreement with me over something." But that is exactly what David did! And it didn't stop there; it got worse. Absalom finally gathered enough support to proclaim himself king of Israel. Now wouldn't you think his father would have confronted him? *No!* Instead, David fled the country in exile, ordering his soldiers not to harm Absalom.

Meanwhile, back at the throne, instead of giving the customary inauguration speech, Absalom pitched a tent on the roof of the palace and had sex with his father's concubines as all Israel watched (see 2 Samuel 16:22)! By now you might be asking yourself, "What the heck was that guy doing?" I'll tell you what he was doing. He was getting revenge on his father for not rescuing Tamar from Amnon, by raping his father's women. He was sending a big, loud message to his dad: "How does it feel when someone violates the girls you care about and you are powerless to help them?"

Absalom was so obsessed with the rape of his sister that he even named his only daughter Tamar after her. In other words, injustice not confronted gives birth to more injustice, ultimately creating legacies of bondage through mindsets of hopelessness.

The Things Giant Killers Fear

Absalom was not King David's only failure. David never confronted any of his sons, resulting in two of them usurping his throne and one raping his daughter. In fact, the king's dysfunction went far beyond the borders of his family. For example, Joab, the commander of David's armies and head of his mighty men, murdered one of Israel's best generals (see 2 Samuel 3:27). But Joab was allowed to retain his post and never even got court-martialed by the king. When Solomon became king, David gave him a hit list of all the people he didn't have the guts to confront when he was in power and ordered the young king to clean up his messes.

The private life of the man after God's heart reads like a disgusting soap opera. But the real question is, what caused a mighty man of God to kill giants, yet not confront his own men? Why would a man have the courage to destroy with his bare hands wild animals that attacked his sheep and take on a nine-foot-six-inch giant with a rock but not discipline his own sons his entire life?

> **The private life of the man**
> **after God's heart reads like**
> **a disgusting soap opera.**

The answer lies in David's formative years as a young solider serving an insane king. King Saul took David from a simple peasant family, moved him into his own royal palace and raised him with his son, Jonathan. But Saul became jealous of his adopted son and spent 14 years trying to kill him. Like many leaders, David reacted to Saul's abusive authority in his life and did the opposite with his sons and soldiers, thus creating a culture in which people were empowered but seldom confronted.

When Sons Become Enemies

After studying the life of David, I began to understand the unhealthy relational component that existed between my two pastor friends. Like David, many leaders hate confrontation. They know how to deal with enemies, but they haven't learned the skills of disciplining their sons and daughters. This often results in leaders and/or fathers being passive *until* their anger finally overcomes their fear of conflict. When the leader has had enough, he usually changes the name of the violator to that of an adversary (Jezebel, Judas and Absalom are the most common) and then they bring their warrior weapons to a family affair. This, of course, never results in reconciliation, because the goal of this kind of conflict is to destroy your enemy and protect the flock from wolves. When the "confrontation" goes bad, it serves to validate that talking to people about their "stuff" leads to the destruction of the relationship. This causes the leader to confront even less, which results in injustice increasing still more, and eventually creates an environment as dysfunctional as King David's family.

As I investigated the relational dynamic between my two pastor friends, I discovered that this same Davidic pattern existed between them from the inception of their friendship. The younger man had a strong personality, but he often lacked communication skills and boundaries. The older leader hated conflict. He was a peacekeeper (again, not to be confused with a peacemaker) and wanted harmony at all costs. But people can only stuff their feelings for so long before they begin to erode from the inside out. The senior leader eventually accumulated a case file so thick that it could no longer be contained in the file drawers of his heart.

When my friend was sent out to plant his own work, the geographic distance between them created a sense of safety for the senior leader to finally articulate his feelings of feeling dishonored, afraid, controlled and run over for almost two decades. But the associate leader had no idea of how he was affecting his environment because he seldom received feedback that wasn't articulated in anger. When his leader was angry with him, he defended himself from his leader's advice instead of assimilating it. Consequently, he grew very little in the areas that were irritations to his mentor. The senior pastor finally concluded that this young man was an enemy, for it is only enemies that "try to hurt people." Thus the Absalom title seemed to fit him perfectly.

Passive Jesus?

Christian leaders tend to spiritualize their dysfunctions by using Scripture that is contextually irrelevant to the core problems of their heart. People who fear confrontation, for instance, often cite Bible verses about turning the other cheek or loving our enemies (see Matthew 5:39,44). But we aren't talking about enemies here. We are talking about family, friends and team members. And we can't afford to ignore the many Scriptures about living a life of confrontation. For example, Proverbs says, "Iron sharpens iron, so one man sharpens another" (Proverbs 27:17) and "Faithful are the wounds of a friend, but deceitful are the kisses of an enemy" (Proverbs 27:6).

> **Christian leaders tend to spiritualize their dysfunctions.**

Some people think Jesus was passive, but nothing could be further from the truth. His words and actions were the most confrontational in the Bible. Let's look at the way Jesus dealt with a few different groups of people. Here is His response to His disciples, who didn't seem to have the faith to cast a demon out of a kid:

> One of the crowd answered Him, "Teacher, I brought You my son, possessed with a spirit which makes him mute; and whenever it seizes him, it slams him to the ground and he foams at the mouth, and grinds his teeth and stiffens out. I told Your disciples to cast it out, and they could not do it." And He answered them and said, "O unbelieving generation, how long shall I be with you? *How long shall I put up with you?* Bring him to Me!" (Mark 9:17-19, emphasis added).

Check out this one! Jesus took exception to some business people selling their stuff at the Temple, so He made a whip and drove them out. Do you think He actually hit anyone? Yikes!

> The Passover of the Jews was near, and Jesus went up to Jerusalem. And He found in the temple those who were selling oxen and sheep and doves, and the money-changers seated at their tables. And He made a scourge of cords, and drove them all out of the temple, with the sheep and the oxen; and He poured out the coins of the money changers and overturned their tables; and to those who were selling the doves He said, "Take these things away; stop making My Father's house a place of business" (John 2:13-16).

But Jesus' favorite target of confrontation was the religious leaders of His day. He didn't have much patience for their self-righteous, ego-centered ministry style:

"Woe to you, scribes and Pharisees, hypocrites! For you clean the outside of the cup and of the dish, but inside they are full of robbery and self-indulgence. You blind Pharisee, first clean the inside of the cup and of the dish, so that the outside of it may become clean also. Woe to you, scribes and Pharisees, hypocrites! For you are like whitewashed tombs which on the outside appear beautiful, but inside they are full of dead men's bones and all uncleanness. So you, too, outwardly appear righteous to men, but inwardly you are full of hypocrisy and lawlessness" (Matthew 23:25-28).

I would like to suggest that Jesus had no problem speaking His mind to people. You always knew where you stood with Him.

The Art of Confrontation

Of course, when Jesus walked the earth, He had a few advantages over us. Minor things like He never sinned, for instance, so He never had to worry about hypocritically pointing out faults in others while neglecting His own. He was also God, and knew the hearts of men; therefore, His assessments of people's motives were always accurate. Undoubtedly, these advantages gave Him confidence and grace when it came to approaching a confrontation; He was neither shy nor overly harsh.

We, on the other hand, have to be told, "Brethren, even if anyone is caught in any trespass, you who are spiritual, restore such a one in a spirit of gentleness; each one looking to yourself, so that you too will not be tempted" (Galatians 6:1). According to this standard, confrontation must never involve yelling at someone, accusing him or her of evil, venting frustration or punishing the person for failing or hurting you. We must be especially careful about not judging the motives of people. In my experience, our so-called "gift of discernment" often turns out to be *suspicion* in disguise, especially when we are upset with someone.

Over the years, I have learned these nine principles for practicing the art of healthy confrontation:

1. When a problem arises, get an appointment to talk to the person as soon as possible. Waiting too long allows the seed of bitterness to gestate. Don't wait for anger to be your counselor. Remember, this is not about punishing the person for his or her inappropriate behavior. You are meeting with the person for his or her benefit. The goal is to help mold the person into the image of God and reconcile your relationship.

2. Let the person know how his or her behavior has affected you. Describe in detail how the person's actions are making you *feel*.

3. Keep your armor off by being transparent about your own struggles. When a person is responding to you, *listen from your heart to his (her) heart*. Many people are not good at articulating their struggles, so you often have to listen beyond their words. As the person is speaking to you, don't develop your defenses or turn the conversation into a war of words. Ask questions that unearth the root problem. What is really wrong? What kind of core problem would cause these symptoms?

4. Always give the person the benefit of the doubt, no matter how he or she has behaved. Remind yourself that the person you are having a problem with was made in the image of God and, therefore, most likely has a good heart, even though his or her behavior is negatively affecting the environment. Never think of the person as an enemy but instead as a wayward son or daughter (father or mother). Show honor at all times. Let the person know you believe in him or her. Remember, you only have as much influence in someone's life as they have value for you.

5. Ask the person how you can be part of the solution. By this time, you may have found out that you are actually part of the problem. Maybe you are King David in this situation. Has your fear, weakness or dysfunction become a seedbed for the person's strength to be overemphasized or his or her weakness to be exposed? Have you reacted to the way you were raised or to some negative circumstances in your own life?

6. If other people are not part of the problem or part of the solution, it is none of their business. Don't talk to other people about your offense with the person. Don't build a case against the person by bringing up other people's names in the conversation, saying things like, "I talked to John and Mary and they have the same problem with you." This just makes you look like a coward and a gossip. If you do that, don't be surprised if the person being

confronted feels like he or she is a victim of a gang assault. You are not there to be someone's attorney.

On this note, if someone comes to you to talk about a problem with someone else, tell him or her to go talk to the person, not to you. I have 357 employees who work for me at Bethel Church. Many of my team members used to come up to me and begin to tell me about a struggle they were having with another staff member. Before they got 20 seconds into their discourse, I would interrupt them and ask, "Have you talked to this person yet?"

Nine out of ten times they would say, "No!"

Then I would ask them, "What business do you have talking to me if you haven't even talked to the person who offended you?"

It is important to remember that a person who talks to you about someone else will one day be talking to someone about you. Allowing people to complain about others creates a culture of gossip. I personally will not tolerate it at Bethel.

It is important to remember that a person who talks to you about someone else will one day be talking to someone about you.

---

7. If you realize during the conversation that you are the problem or a part of the dilemma, be quick to repent. Humility always leads to repentance. Don't defend yourself; leave your weapons outside the door. If the other person is wrong, verbally forgive him or her. Forgiveness restores the standard, so the

person needs to be treated as if he/she never sinned after he or she repents.

Forgiveness restores the standard, so the person needs to be treated as if he/she never sinned after he or she repents.

---

8. If you come to an impasse, have someone you *both* equally respect join you in another meeting to help resolve the issue. Bringing someone into the meeting that is not respected by one of the parties will only feel like the other person's attorney is present. But a wise person who is not emotionally attached to the conflict can bring insightful perspective that is hard to see when you are in the middle of it, and will usually help bring the necessary resolution. I can't count the number of times I've had a problem with someone, only to find out in a meeting with him or her that I am the problem. Having a respected third party present helped me see the truth.

9. Last but not least, don't withdraw from the person after a conflict. Make an extra effort to stay close to him or her during the healing process. This is often the difference between a long healthy relationship and a lifelong pattern of conflict.

A study was completed in the business world many years ago concerning this issue of conflict. The survey showed that when a customer had a problem with a business and the company satisfactorily solved the issue, that customer became many times more loyal to that store in the years that followed than they were before the conflict.

I believe that conflict and confrontation resolved inside the core values of the Kingdom actually strengthen our relationships. These struggles are the sign of real relationships where people feel safe to tell one another the truth in love. This creates covenant societies that bond around family values, instead of fatherless sibling rivalries where orphans vie for preeminence in the pecking order of the world's chicken coop.

"It Takes All Kinds of People to Make the World Go Around"

My mother often said that to me when I was growing up. The older I get, the more I realize she was right. There are black-and-white thinkers like Absalom, who view the world through the lens of justice. They see life as a long journey down the path of wrong and right, good and evil. If someone wired like this witnesses an injustice or is somehow mistreated, he or she often becomes obsessed with the need for closure. If the person lives in an environment where conflict is looked down on or not allowed, he or she tends to come apart inside.

There is an entirely different type of person who views the world in shades of gray. Some of these people just don't like conflict, but others just don't see the need for it. These are the mercy givers of the world who walk in extreme grace. They are not easily offended and they have a high capacity for forgiveness without much articulation. They just naturally trust people, giving them the benefit of the doubt in most situations.

Trouble can arise when you yoke these two extremely different types of people together. I counseled a pastor and his family some years ago where this dynamic had nearly destroyed their family. The pastor was fired from his senior position over some false rumors going around in the church he had planted. He refused to defend himself or his family, believing that the truth would eventually speak for itself. But his 17-year-old son was a justice guy. He needed his dad to step up to the plate and defend the family. When his father refused, he grew angry with him and began to hate the congregation and the Church in general. This young man, who had once been an on-fire leader of his youth group, became a furious, resentful son.

I could see the root of the problem within a few minutes. Mr. Grace was yoked to Mr. Justice in a major conflict, and they each had different needs in order to reach a resolution. The dilemma was finally resolved when I suggested that the family have a meeting with the board that had fired the pastor. In the meeting, the young man was empowered to share how the leadership's decisions had affected him and how unfairly he felt the family was treated. The family went on to pastor another church, and the son became their youth pastor. Sometimes sharing what is on your heart releases you from the need to be right.

Mr. Grace Meets Mr. Justice

Bill Johnson and I have worked together for more than three decades. He is Mr. Grace and I am Mr. Justice. When we have a conflict with someone in our movement, Bill is almost always at the spearhead of mercy. Bill is quick to forgive and restore people to their calling. He believes the best about everyone and rarely says a negative word about anyone. I, Mr. Justice, am pretty quick to forgive, but much slower to trust someone again. Bill tends to trust people until they prove they are not trustworthy. I tend not to trust people until they have earned it.

This difference in perspective has caused some interesting challenges throughout our lives. But the key to our success has been in valuing each other's opinion and listening to one another's perspectives. It is important to remember that just because someone approaches a problem differently than you doesn't make the person wrong. I owe much of my personal success to Bill's gift of mercy. Whenever I have a conflict with Bill's paradigm, I remind myself that it is his mindset that has been the catalyst for my ministry. Bill believed in me before I deserved it! May mercy and truth kiss in the palace of hope.

**May mercy and truth kiss in
the palace of hope.**

7

Casting Vision and Capturing Hearts

If you look at the past long enough,
you will become a monument instead of a movement.
BILL JOHNSON

Imagineers

On December 15, 1966, Walt Disney died, and the world lost one of its greatest Imagineers (Walt's word for dreamers and visionaries). But five years after his death, his greatest dream of all was actualized. Walt Disney had envisioned a theme park so awesome that it created a fantasy world where families could leave the troubles of the outside world behind them.

On October 1, 1971, Walt Disney World officially opened in Orlando, Florida. Walt's brother, Roy, presided over the ribbon-cutting ceremony. In the midst of the celebration, somebody came up to him and said, "It's too bad Walt couldn't be here to see this." Roy responded, "He did see this, and that's why you can see it today."

The author of Hebrews agrees with Roy when it proclaims, "What is seen was not made out of things which are visible" (Hebrews 11:3). This verse speaks of how God creates. He was the original Imagineer, and what He *envisioned* we became. We can also create visible realities from the invisible dimension of our imaginations. In fact, there has never been anything perceived in the visible world that wasn't first assembled in the invisible realm of the imagination.

There has never been anything perceived in the visible world that wasn't first assembled in the invisible realm of the imagination.

Jacob's experience with spotted and speckled sheep, recorded in Genesis 30, illustrates this principle. Jacob worked for his father-in-law, Laban, for a long time. After 14 turbulent years of mistrust and dishonesty, Jacob was ready to leave. He told his father-in-law to give him what was his so he could go his own way. Although Laban was a liar and a cheat, he was no fool. He knew that Jacob was making him a fortune. Laban told Jacob to name his wage and stay working for him. But Jacob knew that no matter what his wages were, his father-in-law would find some way to swindle him out of them. He had to come up with a foolproof plan so Laban couldn't take advantage of him. Finally, Jacob got this crazy idea. He told Laban that he would work for all the spotted and speckled sheep and goats. They struck a deal, and then the story takes on a bizarre twist. Jacob carved spots and speckles in some branches and put them in front of the watering hole whenever the strongest sheep and goats were mating there. What happened next is pretty amazing. Those sheep and goats began giving birth to spotted and speckled offspring!

As I pondered this strange passage, it dawned on me that this was not a lesson in agriculture! It is a parable of how we, *His* sheep, reproduce through our imagination. The watering hole is a place of *reflection*. It represents the place where we imagine, dream and envision the future with God. As we meditate on these ideas, our hearts become "wombs" in which we gestate them like seeds until we give birth to them as offspring.

Mary, the mother of Jesus, experienced this supernatural phenomenon. Dr. Luke writes, "But Mary treasured all these things [the prophetic word the angel gave her about giving birth to the Savior of the world], pondering them in her heart" (Luke 2:19). Mary brooded over the word of God in her heart and gave birth to the Messiah. What she imagined became flesh and, through the Holy Spirit, dwelt among us. In other words, what she perceived in her heart gave her the courage to endure difficulty along the path to her destiny. As human beings, we reach our highest potential when we harness the power of our imagination to birth the realities and purposes of God for us and for the world. When we dream with God, as Mary did, *we* co-create masterpieces of *His* imagination. Bill Johnson captures this supernatural reality so well in his book *Secrets to Imitating God*.

Mary brooded over the word of God in her heart and gave birth to the Messiah.

Vision Gives Pain a Purpose

Of course, I am not saying that if you imagine a pink elephant, you are going to give birth to it. I am simply trying to demonstrate the supernatural principle of envisioning. The New Age movement has been teaching this for years, which has led many Christian leaders to think that the idea is from hell. But the

truth is that New Age leaders are stealing our stuff, and by reacting to them, we have lost the creative power of visioneering.

Okay, now let me be a little more pragmatic for a moment.
This supernatural principle basically works like this: When we
imagine something in our mind's eye, a phenomenon occurs in
our spirit that causes us to want to see with our natural eyes
what we have perceived in our heart. Michelangelo put it like
this: "I saw the angel in the marble and I carved to set it free."
He looked at a boulder with his natural eyes, and with his imagination he pictured an angel imprisoned in the stone. This motivated him to relentlessly chip away at the rock until he could
view on the outside what he imagined on the inside. When people envision something (especially something from God), it creates a naturally supernatural impetus to apprehend the vision
and see it fulfilled, built, funded and otherwise realized.

**Michelangelo put it like this:
"I saw the angel in the marble and
I carved to set it free."**

Solomon said, "Where there is no vision, the people are unrestrained [wander aimlessly], but happy is he who keeps the
law" (Proverbs 29:18). The *King James Version* says it this way:
"Where there is no vision, the people perish: but he that keep-
eth the law, happy is he." When people lack vision, they lead
unrestrained lives. Their life's motivation is reduced to staying out of pain or finding pleasure. This may seem like Easy
Street, but it is actually the path to a mundane, boring existence that ultimately undermines God's divine destiny in their
lives. As Helen Keller, who was blind, said, "It is a terrible thing

to see and have no vision." But when people catch a vision, they will "keep the law"; in other words, they will restrain their options to apprehend their vision. Vision not only gives focused energy that empowers us to say no to certain things and yes to others, but it also gives us the courage to endure difficulties in the path to our destiny.

Let me illustrate. An overweight person goes to the gym to get in shape. But the morning after his first workout, he is so sore that he can hardly get out of bed. If he has a vision (he can picture himself with a great body), that vision will give his pain a purpose. It is vision that causes a person to restrain his eating, reorder his schedule and push past the discomfort of muscle pain to obtain his goal. On the other hand, it is very difficult to get skinny by hating being fat, because reacting to a negative rarely creates a positive.

It is very difficult to get skinny by hating being fat, because reacting to a negative rarely creates a positive.

Vision is the invisible manager that guides, encourages and inspires fervent souls who are undertaking the Master's supernatural assignment to prepare the planet for His reentry. When I see saints exercising enormous self-control, showing great courage in overcoming difficulties and demonstrating excellence in their divine assignments, I know that it means they have captured a vision for their lives.

I am reminded of the old fable of the three bricklayers all working on the same long wall. Someone came up to the first man laying bricks and asked, "Sir, may I ask what you are doing?"

"I am laying bricks," he snapped sarcastically. "What does it look like I am doing?"

The man approached the second bricklayer and asked, "What are you doing?"

"I am building a wall. That's what I am doing."

Finally, the inquisitive onlooker approached the last mason, finding him hard at work, laying bricks with exceptional excellence and speed. "Mister, could I trouble you with a question? What is it that you are doing?" the man asked in admiration.

Still hard at work, the bricklayer answered, "I am building a great cathedral for God."

Which mason would you want working for you?

Vision-Based Discipline

In September 1998, we founded the Bethel School of Supernatural Ministry with 37 students. Over the past 11 years, the school has grown to more than 1,300 full-time students. One of the greatest challenges we have faced over the years is getting students to discipline themselves to come to class on time, do their work, pay their tuition and so on, without creating a controlling environment.

In the early years of our school, I spent many hours with my staff deliberating over different methods of motivating the students. What we realized over time was that most of these ideas were really just systematic levels of punishment dished out to those violating our laws.

Finally, we stumbled upon Solomon's words and realized that it is vision that causes people to keep the law. When people lose their vision, they no longer keep the rules, restrain their options or live disciplined lives. This revelation changed our entire leadership approach to our school. Now, when students act inappropriately, we simply ask them what their vision looks like for their own lives. They rarely can articulate it, because somewhere between the time they decided to make the huge sacrifice required to attend our school and the time they started misbehaving, they lost their vision, the screen went blank, the hard drive crashed and they stopped dreaming.

Thus, our primary goal at that point is to help them rediscover, redeem and re-envision their lives. Often we accomplish this by simply having them recount the story of their journey to the school. Questions like, "What inspired you to come to this supernatural school in the first place? What were you hoping would happen to you when you came here? Share with us in picture form what you thought it was going to look like when you graduated from BSSM." Frequently, there are tears as they recount the vision that motivated them to take the plunge.

Sometimes the treasure of their vision is buried so deep in the soil of disappointment, discouragement or disillusionment that they need help unearthing it. This is where the gifts of the Spirit come in handy. In these situations, we will often ask the Holy Spirit to give us a prophetic word that restores the student's vision and encourages him or her to press past the pain to obtain the prize.

I should make it clear that we do believe in discipline at BSSM (see Hebrews 12:7-12). We understand very well that vision isn't the magical answer to everyone's problem. It is, however, a powerful principle in the hands of the Master Potter.

Imparting Mission and Vision

If we are going to transform cities and make disciples of all nations, we need to capture God's vision for them. One of the struggles I have often encountered in this area is confusion between having a mission and catching a vision. I have often heard leaders use the words "mission" and "vision" interchangeably, as if they are the same thing. But they are not the same thing. Mission is the *why,* the reason or purpose, and the heart motivation behind what we are trying to accomplish. Vision means *what* the mission looks like. It is not really a vision unless you can *see it.* You can do a great job of articulating a mission, but unless people can *see it* in their mind's eye, they remain restrained in their ability to help build it.

> I have often heard leaders use the words "mission" and "vision" interchangeably, as if they are the same thing. But they are not the same thing.

For example, I can tell you all the reasons why we need an orphanage in Kenya, Africa. I can explain to you the extreme negative social conditions that AIDS has created in that country. I can describe to you in detail the destructive nature of poverty that looms heavily over that nation. You may even fly there to help construct the facility. But you can't build a successful structure without seeing the blueprints.

> A leader's ability to envision a mission and then impart it to others is what separates good leaders from great leaders.

A leader's ability to envision a mission and then impart it to others is what separates good leaders from great leaders.

Great leaders have the unique ability to picture the purposes of God in their spirits and then impart the picture to others. You know that people have captured the vision, not when they can repeat it (a parrot can do that), but when they can see it in their spirits. It's *vision* that impregnates people with the need to labor to give birth to a *mission*.

It's *vision* that impregnates people with the need to labor to give birth to a *mission*.

I have watched many times as leaders passionately communicated a mission to people, carefully and meticulously explaining every detail of the purposes behind their plan, but giving their audience no idea what it looks like. Sometimes a mission will capture people's hearts and cause them to give to a project for a season. But sustained, disciplined help usually comes from people who can envision what the mission looks like, because vision motivates them from the inside. Repeating the mission, making fervent pleas or causing people to feel guilty for not making a contribution or a sacrifice is not the way to impart vision. Although these methods may bear some fruit at times, they are most often related to manipulation, which is rooted in witchcraft. Such external motivators never bring out excellence, passion and initiative in people.

The greater the mission is, the clearer the vision must be, because huge assignments usually require high levels of sacrifice and/or risk to see them fulfilled. The level of sacrifice a mission requires determines the measure of clarity necessary for people to follow. When a leader lacks the skill to impart vision, sacrifice begins to separate the people who can instinctively envision from those who can't.

It is for this reason that real estate developers, for example, spend thousands of dollars constructing models of their building ventures in order to help bankers and financiers catch the vision for their projects. Though this adds to the cost of the development, experienced developers realize that investors are not always the greatest visionaries and must be inspired externally. They know that if they can somehow get the financial backers to *see* the project, they are much more likely to take a risk and fund it.

The greater the mission is, the clearer the vision must be.

Leaders need to invest their resources in inspiring faith in their people. It takes faith to capture a grand mission and vision. Without a mission from God, the greatest visions in life are no more than the worthless efforts of self-righteous souls who climb the high mountains of human significance, only to see their passion perish in the thin air of human applause. But without vision, God's holy intentions lay buried in disembodied spirits, His words never become flesh and His righteous purposes remain imprisoned in the small minds of those who refuse to dream with their Creator, and instead bury their talents in the hard soil of comfort and complacency. It is mission that inspires passion and zeal, while vision provokes perseverance and sacrifice.

Seizing the Promised Land

There is another element of vision that leaders must successfully clarify in order to inspire their people to sacrifice for the mission. We see this element in the story of Moses trying to lead the

Israelites into the Promised Land. Moses had to figure out a way to inspire former slaves to capture a vision for a better life on the other side of the river. But the nature of slavery is that you never really learn to dream. The slave nature produces controlling cultures that resist thinking and thus create *dream-free zones.*

> ### The slave nature produces controlling cultures that resist thinking and thus create *dream-free zones.*

Moses' strategy to awaken their imaginations was similar to the real estate developers. He knew the best way to impart vision to slaves was to arouse their five senses with the fruit of their promises. So he sent spies into the Promised Land and commanded them to come back with a detailed report about the land's topography, inhabitants, infrastructure and produce. He also instructed them to make every effort to bring back some fruit from the land:

> When Moses sent them to spy out the land of Canaan, he said to them, "Go up there into the Negev; then go up into the hill country. See what the land is like, and whether the people who live in it are strong or weak, whether they are few or many. How is the land in which they live, is it good or bad? And how are the cities in which they live, are they like open camps or with fortifications? How is the land, is it fat or lean? Are there trees in it or not? Make an effort then to get some of the fruit of the land." Now the time was the time of the first ripe grapes. So they went up and spied out the land

from the wilderness of Zin as far as Rehob, at Lebo-hamath. When they had gone up into the Negev, they came to Hebron where Ahiman, Sheshai and Talmai, the descendants of Anak were. (Now Hebron was built seven years before Zoan in Egypt.) Then they came to the valley of Eshcol and from there cut down a branch with a single cluster of grapes; and they carried it on a pole between two men, with some of the pomegranates and the figs. That place was called the valley of Eshcol, because of the cluster, which the sons of Israel cut down from there. When they returned from spying out the land, at the end of forty days, they proceeded to come to Moses and Aaron and to all the congregation of the sons of Israel in the wilderness of Paran, at Kadesh; and they brought back word to them and to all the congregation and showed them the fruit of the land. Thus they told him, and said, "We went in to the land where you sent us; and it certainly does flow with milk and honey, and this is its fruit" (Numbers 13:17-27).

When the spies returned, reported and displayed the fruit they had brought back, the Israelites heard, saw, felt, smelled and tasted the vision of the Promised Land. Moses did his best to stimulate their five senses so they could imagine the land and give birth to a nation. But 10 spies let their fears dictate their worldview and they sabotaged the purposes of God in the hearts of the people. Here is the account:

Caleb quieted the people before Moses and said, "We should by all means go up and take possession of it, for we will surely overcome it." But the men who had gone up with him said, "We are not able to go up against the people; for they are too strong for us." So they gave out to the sons of Israel a bad report of the land which they had spied out, saying, "The land through which we have gone, in spying it out, is a land that devours its inhabitants; and all the people whom we saw in it are men of great size. There also we saw the Nephilim (the sons of Anak are part of the Nephilim); and we became like grasshoppers in our own sight, and so we were in their sight" (Numbers 13:30-33).

The people, entrenched in their slave mentality, believed the bad report and started talking about going back to Egypt. P. K. Bernard was right when he said, "A man without a vision is a man without a future. A man without a future will always return to his past." People who insist on living in the "good old days" cannot "in-vision." They just don't understand that when your memories are greater than your dreams, you are already dying. Most of the Israelites never did get it. They wandered aimlessly in the wilderness and many of them perished.

A man without a vision is a man without a future. A man without a future will always return to his past.

Their inability to capture the vision was rooted in their failure to embrace their identity as God's covenant people. They forgot the miracles of God in the wilderness and envisioned themselves as grasshoppers in the Promised Land. Low self-esteem will always make you feel like a bug in a land full of giants that are just waiting to squash your dreams.

Unlike the rest of the Israelites, Joshua and Caleb embraced their God-given identity, which allowed God's vision to be etched deeply within their hearts. More than 40 years passed before their dream was realized, yet their hearts still burned for the Promised Land. Here is Caleb's (one of the chief Imagineers of Israel) exhortation to Joshua when they finally entered the land of promise as old men:

> Then the sons of Judah drew near to Joshua in Gilgal, and Caleb the son of Jephunneh the Kenizzite said to him, "You know the word which the LORD spoke to Moses the man of God concerning you and me in Kadesh-barnea. I was forty years old when Moses the servant of the LORD sent me from Kadesh-barnea to spy out the land, and I brought word back to him as it was in my heart. Nevertheless my brethren who went up with me made the heart of the people melt with fear; but I followed the LORD my God fully. So Moses swore on that day, saying, 'Surely the land on which your foot has trodden will be an inheritance to you and to your children forever, because you have followed the LORD my God fully.' Now behold, the LORD has let me live, just as He spoke, these forty-five years, from the time that the LORD spoke this word to Moses, when Israel walked in the wilderness; and now behold, I am eighty-five years old today. I am still as strong today as I was in the day Moses sent me; as my strength was then, so my strength is now, for war and for going out and coming in. Now then, give me this hill country about which the LORD spoke on that day, for you heard on that day that Anakim were there, with great fortified cities; perhaps the LORD will be with me, and I will drive them out as

the LORD has spoken." So Joshua blessed him and gave Hebron to Caleb the son of Jephunneh for an inheritance (Joshua 14:6-13).

The question is: Are you a grasshopper lost in the thorn-infested fields of life or a child of the King, called to destroy the works of the devil?

The question is: Are you a grasshopper lost in the thorn-infested fields of life or a child of the King, called to destroy the works of the devil?

Inspiring a Movement

Movements are always birthed by dreamers who first envision life as it ought to be and not as it is. Dreamers stir people's imaginations, agitate their souls and inspire their hearts. George Bernard Shaw expressed the dreamer's attitude when he said, "Some men see things as they are and ask 'Why?' Others dream of things that never were and ask, 'Why not?'" Dreamers are the cultural catalysts, reformers and history makers. In order for us to experience the fulfillment of the Lord's Prayer, "Your kingdom come Your will be done, on earth as it is in heaven" (Matthew 6:10), it's vital that we begin to envision the world, not as it is, but as it ought to be.

Dr. Martin Luther King is one of the best examples of someone who saw the world the way God intended and altered the course of American history. On August 28, 1963, Dr. King imparted a vision for the equality of all races to an entire generation of people. Although he proclaimed this vision decades ago, it still echoes through the halls of our history. Here is a portion of his speech titled "I Have a Dream":

> Let us not wallow in the valley of despair, I say to you today, my friends.
>
> And so even though we face the difficulties of today and tomorrow, I still have a dream. It is a dream deeply rooted in the American dream.
>
> I have a dream that one day this nation will rise up and live out the true meaning of its creed: "We hold these truths to be self-evident, that all men are created equal."
>
> I have a dream that one day on the red hills of Georgia, the sons of former slaves and the sons of former slave owners will be able to sit down together at the table of brotherhood.
>
> I have a dream that one day even the state of Mississippi, a state sweltering with the heat of injustice, sweltering with the heat of oppression, will be transformed into an oasis of freedom and justice.
>
> I have a dream that my four little children will one day live in a nation where they will not be judged by the color of their skin but by the content of their character.
>
> I have a *dream* today!
>
> I have a dream that one day, down in Alabama, with its vicious racists, with its governor having his lips dripping with the words of "interposition" and "nullification"—one day right there in Alabama little black boys and black girls will be able to join hands with little white boys and white girls as sisters and brothers.
>
> I have a *dream* today!

I have a dream that one day every valley shall be exalted, and every hill and mountain shall be made low, the rough places will be made plain, and the crooked places will be made straight; "and the glory of the Lord shall be revealed and all flesh shall see it together."

This is our hope, and this is the faith that I go back to the South with.

With this faith, we will be able to hew out of the mountain of despair a stone of hope. With this faith, we will be able to transform the jangling discords of our nation into a beautiful symphony of brotherhood. With this faith, we will be able to work together, to pray together, to struggle together, to go to jail together, to stand up for freedom together, knowing that we will be free one day.

It is important to note *how* one of the greatest revolutionaries ever to grace this planet inspired people to sacrifice for the cause. Like an artist, Dr. King used words to paint extraordinary portraits of freedom on the canvas of our imaginations. Every sentence was another stroke of the master's brush, impregnating the minds of his listeners to labor for liberty and struggle for freedom.

Like an artist, Dr. King used words to paint extraordinary portraits of freedom on the canvas of our imaginations.

Dr. King imparted his vision of heaven on earth until the day he died. On April 3, 1968, in Memphis, Tennessee, the day before he was assassinated, Dr. Martin Luther King gave his final public address titled "I Have Been to the Mountaintop." Here is an excerpt from it:

> I left Atlanta this morning, and as we got started on the plane, there were six of us, the pilot said over the public address system, "We are sorry for the delay, but we have Dr. Martin Luther King on the plane. And to be sure that all of the bags were checked, and to be sure that nothing would be wrong with the plane, we had to check out everything carefully. And we've had the plane protected and guarded all night." And then I got to Memphis. And some began to say the threats, or talk about the threats that were out. What would happen to me from some of our sick white brothers?
>
> Well, I don't know what will happen now. We've got some difficult days ahead. But it doesn't matter with me now. *Because I've been to the mountaintop.* And I don't mind. Like anybody, I would like to live a long life. Longevity has its place. But I'm not concerned about that now. I just want to do God's will. *And He's allowed me to go up to the mountain. And I've looked over. And I've seen the Promised Land.* I may not get there with you. But I want you to know tonight, that we, as a people, will get to the Promised Land. And I'm happy, tonight. I'm not worried about anything. I'm not fearing any man. Mine eyes have seen the glory of the coming of the Lord.

Heavy Rain

We need a new generation of people who have the courage of Dr. King to once again rise out of the valley of despair and climb the mountain of revelation. This journey is not for a few chosen people but for a royal race of noblemen. May I remind you of the promise of the day in which we live, a day that began two millennia ago when the apostle Peter quoted the prophet Joel in the book of Acts:

> IT SHALL BE IN THE LAST DAYS, God says, THAT I WILL POUR FORTH OF MY SPIRIT ON ALL MAN-KIND; YOUR SONS AND YOUR DAUGHTERS SHALL PROPHESY, YOUR YOUNG MEN SHALL SEE VISIONS, YOUR OLD MEN SHALL DREAM DREAMS; EVEN ON MY BONDSLAVES, BOTH MEN AND WOMEN, I WILL IN THOSE DAYS POUR FORTH OF MY SPIRIT and they shall prophesy. AND I WILL GRANT WONDERS IN THE SKY ABOVE AND SIGNS ON THE EARTH BELOW, BLOOD, AND FIRE, AND VAPOR OF SMOKE. THE SUN WILL BE TURNED INTO DARKNESS AND THE MOON INTO BLOOD, BEFORE THE GREAT AND GLORIOUS DAY OF THE LORD SHALL COME, AND IT SHALL BE THAT EVERYONE WHO CALLS ON THE NAME OF THE LORD WILL BE SAVED (Acts 2:17-21).

In these last days, God promises to pour out His Spirit on *everyone!* One of the main manifestations of this *heavy rain* is that old folks begin to dream again while God infuses young people with His visions. Supernatural vision and God-inspired dreams are freely available to all who will seek this outpouring. And with more than 4 billion lost people on this planet, there has never been a more urgent need for Kingdom Imagineers, royal people and radical visionaries who sit in heavenly places with Christ and dream with God. It's time we stop complaining about our circumstances and journey to the top of the mountain. It is from these heights that we will envision the world, not as it is, but as God intended it to be.

I want to ask you again: What would your city look like if the kingdom of God were superimposed over every realm of society? Can you imagine what would happen to the crime rate, the divorce rate, terminal diseases, hate, abortion, depression, poverty, hopelessness, molestation, rape, pornography, addictions, unemployment . . . if you and other dreamers began to envision the future of your city with God, and then impregnated the populace with that vision like Martin Luther King did in his day?

**What would your city look like if
the kingdom of God were superimposed over
every realm of society?**

Dreamers and visionaries, take your places in the downpour of the Spirit's rain and let it fill the pores of your soul with hope that feels, faith that sees and love that never fails!

8

Impregnating
the Cosmos

Prophecy is history written in advance.
GRAHAM COOKE

Creating the Future

The year is 907 B.C., and Israel's king has managed to lead them away from God into idolatry. His name is Jeroboam. He begins his reign by setting up two golden calves and demanding that his people worship them instead of Jehovah. In the midst of the king's insanity, an unnamed prophet steps onto the scene and somehow manages to get into the king's presence. The prophet rebukes Jeroboam and declares that another king named Josiah is coming to restore Israel back to God. He prophesies to the wicked altar Jeroboam has built, saying that Josiah will sacrifice its evil priests upon it (see 1 Kings 13:2). Then he puts an exclamation point on his declaration: "This is the sign which the LORD has spoken, 'Behold, the altar shall be split apart and the ashes which are on it shall be poured out'" (1 Kings 13:3).

King Jeroboam stretches out his hand, yelling, "Seize him" (1 Kings 13:4), and his arm becomes paralyzed and hangs useless by his side. The prophet calls for God to heal the king, and God restores him. The man of God exits the place a little heated as the altar splits in half and the ashes pour out (see 1 Kings 12–13).

Josiah

Two hundred and seventy years pass, and things continue to decline in Judah. King Manasseh's 55-year reign of terror plunges the country into one of the darkest seasons in their history. Thousands of children are sacrificed on the altars of idols, and the streets of Israel are filled with blood. No end to the bloodshed seems to be in sight when Manasseh's son Amon takes the throne after his father's death and continues to carry out his evil agenda. But then, two years into Amon's reign, he is assassinated (see 2 Kings 21:19-24). This is where the plot thickens.

It's now 640 B.C., and Josiah is crowned king at eight years old. When he turns 26, for some seemingly unknown reason, he begins to seek the Lord, breaking generational curses passed down to him by his father and grandfather. Josiah calls for the restoration of the house of the LORD, which hasn't been used in more than half a century. In the middle of the renovation project, Hilkiah, the high priest, finds a Bible hidden in the Temple someplace, one of the only copies to survive Manasseh's reign of terror. Hilkiah gives the Book to Shaphan the scribe, who rushes into the king's chambers and reads it to Josiah. Second Kings 22:11 says, "When the king heard the words of the book of the law, he tore his clothes." From that point on, Josiah becomes a radical revivalist. He tears down the altars of Baal, destroys the evil priesthood, burns everything dedicated to the worship of other gods and calls the nation back to Jehovah.

But what really happened on that fateful day when, for the first time in Josiah's life, he heard the Word of God? Well, some things are clear. The king realized how far Judah had fallen from God's standard and how badly they deserved to be judged. But something else happened. Josiah not only heard the Word of God for Judah, but he also received a prophetic word for himself. He embraced the declaration and seized his destiny—

all because a prophet had looked into the future and called something that was not as though it was:

> Furthermore, the altar that was at Bethel and the high place which Jeroboam the son of Nebat, who made Israel sin, had made, even that altar and the high place he broke down. Then he demolished its stones, ground them to dust, and burned the Asherah. Now when Josiah turned, he saw the graves that were there on the mountain, and he sent and took the bones from the graves and burned them on the altar and defiled it according to the word of the LORD which the man of God proclaimed, who proclaimed these things (2 Kings 23:15-16).

Imagine what it must have been like for Josiah to realize that a prophet had called him by name and declared his destiny hundreds of years before he was born. When he heard the word, Josiah understood that he had a God-given destiny, that his life was not an accident or just the fruit of an intimate moment between his parents. No, he had a race to run, a purpose to fulfill and a mark to make for God. He was alive somewhere in the heart of God years before he came forth into this world, and it was his appointed time to challenge an ungodly system and make history (see 2 Kings 22–23).

Words Become Worlds

Now let's fast-forward about another 700 years. Peter and John are right outside the gate called Beautiful that leads to the Temple. A man, lame from birth, is sitting at the entrance of the gate. He is begging for money, but the apostles are broke. So

Peter grabs the guy, pulls him to his feet and commands him to walk. You know the rest of the story—the lame man gets completely healed and starts going nuts. A bunch of people gather around, trying to figure out what all the commotion is about. Peter takes the opportunity to preach to the crowd. At the end of his message he makes this statement:

> All the prophets who have spoken, from Samuel and his successors onward, also announced these days. It is you who are the sons of the prophets and of the covenant which God made with your fathers, saying to Abraham, "AND IN YOUR SEED ALL THE FAMILIES OF THE EARTH SHALL BE BLESSED" (Acts 3:24-25).

What did Peter mean, "It is you who are the sons of the prophets"? I'll tell you what he was saying. He was teaching us how history becomes *His*-story. He was saying that the prophet Samuel and all the prophets after him looked into the future and saw a race of people who had never graced this planet before. As they perceived them, they began to prophesy about them. Their prophecies impregnated the "womb of the dawn" (Psalm 110:3), if you will, with the "sperm" of God Himself. A completely new species of being was born from their prophetic declarations. Just like the days of Jeroboam, when the unnamed prophet spoke of a king named Josiah, Samuel and successors also saw us and called us into being.

Let me see if I can make this principle a little clearer. Jesus told a parable about a sower who planted seed in different types of soil. He said that the seed was the Word of God and the soil was our hearts in varying conditions (see Matthew 13:3-23). The Greek word "seed" in this text is the word *sperma*, from which we get the English word "sperm." When the Word of the

Lord is released into our hearts, we become impregnated with the Father's DNA and give birth to His nature in our lives. Paul referred to this when he wrote, "My children, with whom I am again in labor until Christ is formed in you" (Galatians 4:19). How did Paul labor among them? He preached the Word of God, and as he spoke they were impregnated with the seeds of the Kingdom, which literally caused Christ to be formed in them.

As the prophets, Samuel and his successors, prophesied into the future, they impregnated the atmosphere with the seed of God, which in turn created a kind of gestation in creation itself. That's why Romans says, "For we know that the whole creation groans and suffers the pains of childbirth together until now" (Romans 8:22). Jesus spoke of world tribulation that would take place at the *end of the age,* saying, "But all these things are merely the beginning of birth pangs" (Matthew 24:8). Creation itself is in labor as it is giving birth to the heirs of salvation. The head is crowning just in time; the world, groaning in the hope of redemption, will be delivered from this present darkness.

The head is crowning just in time; the world, groaning in the hope of redemption, will be delivered from this present darkness.

The Israel of God

Before we uncover some of the prophetic declarations that have impregnated the cosmos, it's important that we understand that most of the promises, proclamations and prophecies that were made over Israel belong to the entire Body of Christ, not just to those who are born of natural Jewish decent. Paul said that Jesus has reconciled the Gentiles, who were once strangers to the *promises,* into one body, blending us with natural Jewish believers through the cross (see Ephesians 2:11-16). The "promises" are the fruit of the prophetic declarations made by God through Old Testament prophets. Paul goes on to say that the Spirit creates Jews through the circumcision of the heart, not by birthplace, genealogies, or the efforts of men:

> For he is not a Jew who is one outwardly, nor is circumcision that which is outward in the flesh. But he is a Jew who is one inwardly; and circumcision is that which is of the heart, by the Spirit, not by the letter (Romans 2:28-29).

> It is not the children of the flesh who are children of God, but the children of the promise are regarded as descendants (Romans 9:8).

Writing to the believers in Rome, many of whom were Gentiles, of course, Paul said, "For whatever was written in earlier times was written for our instruction, so that through perseverance and the encouragement of the Scriptures we might have hope" (Romans 15:4). This implies that what was written in the Old Testament was penned for the benefit of all believers, not just those born of Jewish origin. Paul goes on to make radical statements to the Galatians, telling them, "Neither is circumcision anything, nor uncircumcision, but a new creation. And those who will walk by this rule, peace and mercy be upon them, and upon the Israel of God" (Galatians 6:15-16). He also said, "The Jerusalem above is free; she is our mother" (Galatians 4:26). Christians, both Jew and Gentile, are the Israel of God, and the New Jerusalem is our mother, our place of origin. Thus, although it is evident that some of the Old Testament promises have single-dimensional fulfillment in the nation of natural Israel alone, most of them have powerful secondary ramifications for all Christians. We are not trying to steal natural Israel's promises; we are simply borrowing them eternally as a part of the adopted cosmic family of God!

Becoming the Proclamations

Let's look at a few of the prophetic declarations, promises and provisions given to us by God. He spoke to Abraham about a time when his descendants would benefit *all* the nations of the earth. He said, "I will multiply your descendants as the stars of heaven, and will give your descendants all these lands; and by your descendants all the nations of the earth shall be blessed" (Genesis 26:4). The birth of Christ in the lineage of Abraham initiated the fulfillment of this promise, but I am sure it is obvious that this declaration still lingers in the halls of history as the world waits for it to be fulfilled in the Body of Christ.

Ezekiel looked into the future and prophesied about a people who would have a new heart and a new spirit (see Ezekiel 36:26). This is why the person who is least in the kingdom of God is superior to John the Baptist, who was the greatest Old Testament prophet ever to set foot on this planet.

The prophet Zechariah spoke of a people who were so great that the feeblest among them would be like King David, and the house of David would be like God Himself (see Zechariah 12:8). Maybe that's why Jesus promised, "He who believes in Me, the works that I do, he will do also; and greater works than these he will do; because I go to the Father" (John 14:12).

The writer of Hebrews grabbed an Old Testament prophecy out of the book of Jeremiah and pulled it into the New Covenant. Jeremiah wrote:

"They will not teach again, each man his neighbor and each man his brother, saying, 'Know the LORD,' for they will all know Me, from the least of them to the greatest of them," declares the LORD, "for I will forgive their iniquity, and their sin I will remember no more" (Jeremiah 31:34; see also Hebrews 8:11-12).

Just imagine, envision and dream about a time when everyone knows the Lord because He has inscribed His words on their hearts. Here is one of my favorite prophecies in the entire Bible:

Now it will come about that in the last days the mountain of the house of the LORD will be established as the chief of the mountains, and will be raised above the hills; and all the nations will stream to it. And many peoples will come and say, "Come, let us go up to the mountain of the LORD, to the house of the God of Jacob; that He may teach us concerning His ways and that we may walk in His paths." For the law will go forth from Zion and the word of the LORD from Jerusalem. And He will judge between the nations, and will render decisions for many peoples; and they will hammer their swords into plowshares and their spears into pruning hooks. Nation will not lift up sword against nation, and never again will they learn war (Isaiah 2:2-4).

Meditate on those verses for a while and they will make you happy! Nations are no longer going to be at war with each other because they are going to come to the house of the Lord and learn God's ways. Could this result, for example, in nations remodeling their weapons plants into factories that generate fresh produce to feed the world? It totally makes sense when you compare Isaiah's prophecy with the commission that Jesus gave us to make disciples of *all nations* and then teach them everything He taught us (see Matthew 28:19-20). This could be one of the ways that we are to be a blessing to all the countries in the world.

Prophetic words become catalytic agents that mold the events of our lives, personally and corporately, into a beautiful tapestry of historic exploits.

The Process of Pro-Creation

There are hundreds of verses that Samuel and his successors prophesied concerning us. It would take an entire book just to investigate a few of them. But the purpose of this chapter is simply to point out how God turns history into His-story. The Lord gives His prophets and prophetic people timeless insights. These history makers take these insights and they proclaim them into the cosmos, impregnating the atmosphere with destiny and purpose. These prophetic words become catalytic agents that mold the events of our lives, personally and corporately, into a beautiful tapestry of historic exploits. The outcome is that these hidden mysteries that lie deep in the heart of the Father begin to be painted on the canvas of time.

Running Out of Time

Let's fast-forward again to the year 1970, when a dramatic shift took place in our worldview. A book was published titled *The Late Great Planet Earth*. This book helped to popularize an eschatology that changed the Church's message from "The Kingdom is at hand" to "The end of the world is near." It assisted in creating an expectation for the Antichrist to institute the destructive nature of the "Beast" and his deceptive mark. This resulted in a kind of "Beam Me Up, Scotty" theology in most Christians as we began to anticipate a sudden cosmic rescue. (Let me be clear that Hal Lindsey, the author of the book, simply put words to an end-time view that was already popular in the Jesus Movement, and like all of us in every epoch season, he was operating out of the revelation revealed to his generation.)

One of the main verses shouted in this eschatology was, "But woe to them that are with child, and to them that give suck in those days!" (Mark 13:17, *KJV*). Is it a coincidence that three years after this book was published, *Roe v. Wade* passed the Supreme Court and it became legal to take the life of our unborn in every state in America? Is it possible that many misguided people considered abortion some sort of mercy killing? Could it be that some people couldn't bear the thought of bringing a child into a world where the Antichrist would make them take a number or torture them into compliance?

> Is it possible that many misguided people considered abortion some sort of mercy killing?

You might be asking, "Where was the Church during these crucial Supreme Court proceedings?" I'll tell you where we were: We were waiting for the Rapture! Our eschatology taught us that there was not supposed to be a future. I personally never went to college, because I didn't want to "waste my time" on something that was "all going to burn," as we commonly used to say.

Here is another interesting side note. I was born January 31, 1955, the same year Steve Jobs and Bill Gates were born. Bill Joy was born in November 1954. These men were some of the main catalysts that birthed the Information Age. Few, if any, of the people who ushered in the Information Age were followers of Jesus Christ. Steve Jobs was a Buddhist, Bill Gates is an agnostic, Michael Dell is Jewish, and I am not sure about Bill Joy. "So what's the point?" you ask. Well, have you ever wondered why there was hardly a single Christian at the forefront of the emerging Information Age? I believe it's because the Jesus Movement, which largely embraced the *Late Great* eschatology, was birthed at the same time. Christian young people were all waiting for the great escape, leaving their non-Christian peers to follow the *kairos* clock of the Information Age and become the forerunners of the new epoch season. There were no Christian forerunners because there were no forethinkers. We were all taught to live for eternity, but no one seemed to understand that we were also supposed to live *from* eternity. Let me explain.

There were no Christian forerunners
because there were no forethinkers.
We were all taught to live for eternity, but no
one seemed to understand that we were also
supposed to live from eternity.

Someone Hijacked History

Could it be that the worst element of this end-time paradigm is that it helps to empower a dethroned devil to steal our children's future? By now you are probably saying, "Kris, what the heck are you talking about?" Remember what I shared with you in the beginning of this chapter? The way God creates history is by anointing people to see the future from His perspective and call it into existence (see Romans 4:17). Then, like Josiah and Peter, each generation steps into their destiny by fulfilling the words that were prophesied over them in the past. But part of each generation's destiny is to keep the voice of the Lord alive by prophesying destiny over the generations to come. Just as Jesus said to the apostle John, "Come up here, and I will show you what must take place after these things" (Revelation 4:1), God invites us to sit with Him in heavenly places, where we can see from His perspective what He wants to take place in the future. It is from this posture that we can prophesy *from eternity* because we received foresight and insight that is being empowered by His-sight. Our words become worlds, and history is transformed into His-story. Thus, we become the answers to the prayers and prophecies of Samuel and his successors, and we also join the ranks of successors by releasing our own prayers and prophecies over our future generations.

> **The way God creates history is by anointing people to see the future from His perspective and call it into existence.**

But what happened to destiny when our prophetic people were taught that there wasn't supposed to be a future because the end of the world was near? They stopped prophesying into the future. And what took place in the absence of the Holy Spirit's prophetic intonation is absolutely frightening; a visionary vortex, or vacuum, was suddenly created that sucked every kind of dark foretelling spirit into it. This has resulted in the worst psychic resurgence since the days of Daniel. We have Wiccans, New Age people, fortunetellers, astrologers and psychics all sharing their insights in some of the highest offices in our land. It has become an accepted practice to employ these second-heaven revelators to help prevent crimes and solve problems. The office of Homeland Security, the FBI, CIA and even our local police forces are all employing them. Of course, it isn't hard for psychics to have insight into the crimes that their boss plotted, planned and inspired.

We can prophesy from eternity because we received foresight and insight that is being empowered by His-sight.

Not only is a vacuum of true prophetic declarations creating a crisis in history, but our enemy has taken over our abandoned role of declaring destiny and is perpetuating his diabolical schemes on our planet. As long as we shirk our commission to destroy the works of the devil (see John 10:10; 1 John 3:8), we fail to arrest his mission to kill, steal and destroy.

Our Legacy

We must consider the fact that our eschatology could be robbing us of our legacy. Remember, "The secret things belong to the LORD our God, but the things revealed belong to us and to our sons forever" (Deuteronomy 29:29). Prophetic revelation unlocks the hidden treasures that are to be handed down from generation to generation. But in order for us to prophesy the future and thus lay a foundation for a multigenerational inheritance, we must believe that there is supposed to be a future.

> **We must consider the fact that
> our eschatology could be robbing
> us of our legacy.**

In the winter of 2007, the Lord spoke to me, saying, "The spirit of fatalism and the spirit of martyrdom are holding back the apostolic age." Fatalism refuses to acknowledge positive advancement on the earth and looks for the world to erode instead of evolve. It forces Scriptures such as "there will be no end to the increase of His government or of peace" (Isaiah 9:7) into a distant future time zone that prevents them from inspiring hope for the coming generations. The Church is notorious for using fear as a primary motivator to get people to come into the Kingdom. We need to make sure that we don't build partnership with terrorist spirits, believing we can drive people to God, because there is no fear in love, and it is actually the kindness of God that leads us to repentance (see Romans 2:4). So it is very difficult to keep people in the Kingdom who have been driven there predominantly by a fatalist eschatology.

> **The spirit of fatalism and the
> spirit of martyrdom are holding
> back the apostolic age.**

Martyrdom embraces death in a sadistic way and values the cross above the joy set before us. Jesus *endured* the cross; He didn't enjoy it! When it was His time to die, He even prayed, "Father, if You are willing, remove this cup from Me" (Luke 22:42).

Martyrdom embraces death in a sadistic way and values the cross above the joy set before us. Jesus *endured* the cross; He didn't enjoy it!

An Apostolic Eschatology

The Lord went on to tell me that He was going to give us an "apostolic eschatology." In the preceding chapters, we explored the mission of a true apostle. I talked about the fact that apostolic ministry is synonymous with cultural transformation. We know that the only prayer Jesus ever taught us to pray includes the phrase that the Kingdom would come "on earth as it is in heaven." Therefore, the first question we have to ask ourselves is this: "Did Jesus teach us to pray a prayer that He never intended us to believe?" I think we can agree that the answer to that question is *no!* If we are to pray that it would be on earth as it is in heaven, and if we are commissioned to "make disciples of all the nations" (Matthew 28:19), then doesn't it stand to reason that we need a new approach to the end times?

Did Jesus teach us to pray a prayer that He never intended us to believe?

What we believe about the end has a lot to do with how we behave in the middle. For example, say I have a 1955 Chevy, and you have an automotive restoration shop. Imagine that I take my car into your shop to be rebuilt from the ground up and I inform you that money is no object. But in the middle of the restoration project, you discover that I am going to enter the old Chevy in the destruction derby after you complete the project. That information is definitely going to affect the quality of your work!

What we believe about the end has a lot to do with how we behave in the middle.

In the same way, any reasonable person should be able to figure out that their end-time perspective can dramatically affect the quality of their daily lives. Once again, Isaiah prophesied that the Spirit of the Lord has anointed us to see freedom and restoration come into people's lives and described how *their* personal restoration would result in cities and nations being rebuilt. He wrote, "Then they will rebuild the ancient ruins, they will raise up the former devastations; and they will repair the ruined cities, the desolations of many generations" (Isaiah 61:4). It is difficult to feel empowered to restore ruined cities and at the same time believe that the condition of the world needs to erode for Jesus to return. Can you see that our eschatology is actually working against our ministry? Jack Taylor put it this way: "It's hard to give people heaven by the half acre while believing that things are going to hell in a hand basket." I wonder if it is possible that we are actually on the eve of construction?

The Plight of Creation Care

This point was brought to my mind again recently when I was invited to a roundtable summit where several hundred leaders gathered to discuss the diverse challenges of cultural transformation. The purpose of the conference was to find creative solutions for the world's problems. The event was divided into several topics that we had the privilege of dialoguing about. Ecology, or Creation Care, was one of the main themes of our discussion.

Different leaders passionately debated the subject as several of us listened attentively. One speaker pointed out that cultivating the planet was the first responsibility that God gave to Adam personally and the second command He gave to man corporately (see Genesis 1:20-31; 2:15—the first corporate commission was, "Be fruitful and multiply"). Another individual expounded on the fact that the New Age movement is leading the Green revolution and that Christians are decades behind the rest of the world on the subject. That comment inspired a couple of hours of dialogue as several bright Christian scientists and ecologists weighed in on the matter.

Our eschatology seems to be undermining our ecology.

As the dialogue went on, I had this thought: *There is an elephant in the room and nobody wants to talk about it. Our eschatology seems to be undermining our ecology.* The planet, metaphorically speaking, is our '55 Chevy, and the Church is God's restoration shop. Peter put it like this:

> Therefore repent and return, so that your sins may be wiped away, in order that times of refreshing may come from the presence of the Lord; and that He may send Jesus, the Christ appointed for you, whom heaven must

receive until the period of restoration of all things about which God spoke by the mouth of His holy prophets from ancient time (Acts 3:19-21).

As I have mentioned several times already, we are called to bring heaven to earth and thus become the catalyst for the restoration of all things. But it is hard to get excited about the ministry of restoration or the promise of the meek inheriting the earth while envisioning a Cajun-cooked planet!

Light and Darkness

For years, I preached that in the Last Days the light is going to get brighter and brighter while the darkness gets darker and darker. Then one day I had this revelation: light and darkness cannot cohabit. It is scientifically impossible to increase the light in a room and have it simultaneously get darker—unless you shield the light with something. The only other way to have light and darkness intensify concurrently is to confine or limit the light to a certain geographic or demographic location. But Jesus said:

> You are the light of the world. A city set on a hill cannot be hidden; nor does anyone light a lamp and put it under a basket, but on the lampstand, and it gives light to all who are in the house. Let your light shine before men in such a way that they may see your good works, and glorify your Father who is in heaven (Matthew 5:14-16).

Jesus made it clear that we are the light of the entire *world*. Our light is to be placed in the highest, most visible location possible in each of our cities. It is never to be hidden under a basket or shielded by an object.

If this is true, then it should inspire many questions in our hearts. For example: What about all the verses in the New Testament that speak about the terrible times that are coming in the Last Days? Good question. Here are a few possible explanations. First, we have to understand that the phrase "the last days" spans thousands of years, beginning with Peter's proclamation in Acts 2:17 and extending to the return of Jesus. The Bible refers to several different kinds of events as well as various epoch season changes taking place in the midst of this timeline called the Last Days. Some of them are very bad and dark, while others are amazing and full of light. We have, for example, Scripture like 2 Timothy, where Paul writes to instruct his disciple on how he should respond to evil people in the Last Days:

> But realize this, that in the last days difficult times will come. For men will be lovers of self, lovers of money, boastful, arrogant, revilers, disobedient to parents, ungrateful, unholy, unloving, irreconcilable, malicious gossips, without self-control, brutal, haters of good, treacherous, reckless, conceited, lovers of pleasure rather than lovers of God, holding to a form of godliness, although they have denied its power; avoid such men as these (2 Timothy 3:1-5).

The real question is: Where do these verses belong in the timeline of "the last days"? A couple things come to mind. First of all, it is clear that Paul expected Timothy to be experiencing these things in his day. He gives him *personal* instruction about how to deal with people bent on evil. In other words, he wasn't necessarily giving Timothy a commentary on the condition of the planet at the return of Jesus; he could have been exhorting him about the days in which they currently lived. Therefore, my question is, when we see people in this evil condition living around us, does it really prove that things are getting worse?

In order to understand the full counsel of God when we are developing an end-time mindset, we must embrace all Scripture that deal with the Last Days, like this one in the book of Isaiah:

> Arise, shine; for your light has come, and the glory of the LORD has risen upon you. For behold, darkness will cover the earth and deep darkness the peoples; but the LORD will rise upon you and His glory will appear upon you. Nations will come to your light, and kings to the brightness of your rising. Lift up your eyes round about and see; they all gather together, they come to you. Your sons will come from afar, and your daughters will be carried in the arms. Then you will see and be radiant, and your heart will thrill and rejoice; because the abundance of the sea will be turned to you, the wealth of the nations will come to you (Isaiah 60:1-5).

Notice that God exhorts us to arise in the midst of the deep darkness that is upon the people and begin to shine. This positive posture of arising results in nations, kings and people coming from around the world to be healed, saved, delivered and transformed. Their condition is so desperate that they are willing to offer all their wealth to the people of God in exchange for their darkened condition being enlightened. I think that Scripture like Paul's exhortation to Timothy, for example, could be a perfect description of the deep darkness that the Church has been commanded to arise and shine in. Is it possible that the outcome of the Body of Christ shining in the midst of the worst conditions on the planet isn't that evil somehow increases, but that it is destroyed?

End-Time Thoughts

It would take an entire book to do any justice to the subject of the end times. Harold Eberle and Martin Trench have written a great book titled *Victorious Eschatology*. They have some fresh perspectives and real insights into the Scriptures dealing with this subject. I recommend that you read it with an open mind. Their book covers Jesus' "end of the age" prophecy in Matthew 24, and also gives a refreshing perspective on the book of Revelation. For whatever it's worth, their book did not inspire this chapter. I have held this positive eschatological view for many years. It was, however, inspiring to find other leaders sharing a victorious understanding of the Last Days.

> **Your eschatological core values**
> **could be affecting your ministry,**
> **and more importantly, your legacy.**

The goal of my book is not to give you another chart to argue over or to enter into a theological debate on the various views of end-time prophecy. I simply want to challenge your thinking. I want you to be aware that, like it or not, your eschatological core values could be affecting your ministry, and more importantly, your legacy. We owe it to our children's children's children to have the courage to question old paradigms that could rob hope from the coming generations. Hope is the seedbed that faith grows in, and faith is what Jesus is looking for when He returns to the planet: "When the Son of Man comes, will He find faith on the earth?" (Luke 18:8).

Bill Johnson says, "To think that things are going to get worse and worse in the last days takes no faith." What is more, desiring Jesus to return now relegates billions of people to hell. Peter understood this when he said, "The Lord is not slow about His promise, as some count slowness, but is patient toward you, not wishing for any to perish but for all to come to repentance" (2 Peter 3:9). It's so important that we put on the mind of Christ and do not let our *circumstances* dictate our *stances*. Every time we react to the world's condition instead of responding in faith, we find ourselves *under* the circumstances. A lot of bad doctrine comes out of a sense of powerless Christianity. We tend to spiritualize our dysfunction, mask our fears and excuse our inability to see greater works happen through our lives.

**A lot of bad doctrine comes out of a
sense of powerless Christianity.**

I am personally on an eschatological journey. I feel like Abram when he first met God. The Lord told him to leave his country and journey to a land He would show him (see Genesis 12:1). Abram didn't know where he was going; he just knew where he couldn't stay. I know I can't stay in the end-time theology that is stealing my children's future, instilling fear as a primary motivation for serving the Father and undermining the Great Commission to make disciples of *all* nations.

**Abram didn't know where he was going;
he just knew where he couldn't stay.**

Even though I am not sure where I am going, I have decided to allow a few simple core values to determine my eschatological journey. First, I will not let mystical passages that have been debated for centuries undermine the clear commands, promises and prophecies we have from the Lord Himself, many of which I have already discussed at length in this book. Second, I will not embrace an end-time view that diminishes hope, promotes fear or re-arms the same devil that Jesus disarmed on the cross (see Colossians 2:13-15).

> **I will not embrace an end-time view that diminishes hope, promotes fear or re-arms the same devil that Jesus disarmed on the cross.**

The book of Revelation was written to be the revelation of Jesus Christ, not the revelation of the Antichrist (see Revelation 1:1). The book of Revelation was penned in a prophetic style common to the mystics and it is, therefore, prone to subjectivity. I won't allow its interpretation to promote powerless Christianity. The command that has been passed down from generation to generation with growing momentum is to destroy the works of the devil (see 1 John 3:8). It remains true in every epoch season in life that when we submit to God and resist the devil, he flees from us (see James 4:7). Therefore, I will not embrace an eschatology that undermines our commission to make disciples of all nations or deters our mandate to restore our ruined cities.

> **I will not embrace an eschatology that undermines our comission to make disciples of all nations.**

Finally, I won't believe any end-time interpretation of Scripture that redefines the nature of God. He is good all the time. His love for us is indescribable, incomprehensible, unimaginable and impossible to exaggerate. His mercy runs deeper than the ocean, His compassion is wider than the sea, and His thoughts toward us are innumerable. He created us for His pleasure and, therefore, He enjoys being with us.

> I won't believe any end-time interpretation of Scripture that redefines the nature of God.

With all of that being said, there are still Scriptures that seem to point to another perspective that is very pessimistic and can't be ignored. It is therefore my conviction that, more than ever, we need the Holy Spirit to lead us into all truth and guide us through these theological minefields in our eschatological journey. May God give us wisdom and insight for the times that we live in; and may we, together, find the Promised Land of our souls.

9

A Wonderful World

Sometimes things that are too good to be true are true!
KRIS VALLOTTON

For Goodness' Sake

In 1968, Louis Armstrong, an African American basking in the fresh flame of the civil rights movement, stared down the doomsayers of his era when he sang the famous song "What a Wonderful World." Here is a line from the song:

> I see trees of green, red roses too, I see them bloom
>   for me and you
> And I think to myself, what a wonderful world.[1]

A couple of years ago, I downloaded the song onto my iPod and happened to listen to it for the first time during a flight on my way to a conference. The song unearthed a crisis in my soul, one so deep that I was unaware it even existed. As the song played, I found myself in a battle that is impossible to explain accurately with mere words, but I will try. My heart wrenched with every line of the lyrics as my mind engaged in a heated conflict within itself. My brain became a battlefield and various Scriptures emerged as soldiers warring against one another in a kind of noble struggle for truth. I kept pushing replay on my iPod, because it felt like Louis's words were reinforcements in my war for reality. As the hours passed, I came to understand that a foreboding spirit (foreboding means an impending sense of doom) had somehow lodged itself in my soul and was dictating my worldview. I realized that there was some sort of warped need in me to believe that things were getting worse in the world.

> I came to understand that a foreboding spirit had somehow lodged itself in my soul and was dictating my worldview.

The Terrible Truth About the Improving State of the World

There I was, flying halfway around the world on a 12-hour flight aboard an air-conditioned jet, thousands of miles from home, making a journey that only a century ago would have taken a year on horseback or months on a ship, and would have been incalculably more dangerous.

The war in my mind intensified, so I decided to retreat to a movie for a couple hours of solace. I adjusted the TV screen in front of me and began to check out the selection. As I flipped through the entertainment choices, I was frustrated that they seemed a bit dated. I had already watched most of the 10 movies the airline offered. The other shows were chick-flicks, and I was not desperate enough to cry through a movie for entertainment. I grumbled to myself about how badly the financial crisis had affected the transportation industry. Just then, I remembered that I had brought a DVD with me. I opened my laptop, put my Bose noise-canceling headset on, and inserted the movie.

By now, all this stress was giving me the munchies, so I pushed the button to alert the flight attendant that I needed attention. She came over to my seat and just happened to have my favorite soda in her cart. I asked her for something to eat. She showed me a menu and informed me that I would have to pay $5 for a meal. "Five dollars!" I whined. "What is happening to this world?" She explained to me that things were really tough in the airline business, so they had to charge for stuff they used to give away. I moaned a little more, pulled out my American Express card, and charged the meal.

When we finally landed, I called Kathy on my cell phone to let her know I had arrived safely. We talked for a while and she informed me that the water district had raised our rates 20 percent due to the severe drought conditions that were hammering Northern California. She went on to suggest that we cut back on watering our lawn. "I want our lawn to stay green," I protested. When we hung up the phone, I thought to myself, *Global warming is already killing my lawn!*

Global warming is already killing my lawn!

My host was at the baggage claim to pick me up when I arrived. It was really hot outside, but he had kept the car running, so the vehicle was a cool 70 degrees when I got in. He asked if I had been able to sleep on my 12-hour international flight. "No," I complained. "It was a hard flight. I had to ride in the cattle car seats." We stopped at Starbucks to get a $4 cup of coffee on the way to our hotel. As he drove, I pulled out *USA Today* and began to read. The bad news regarding the 7 billion people who inhabit this planet filled several pages of the paper. I felt terrible for Tiger Woods's family as the story of his affairs, which had been unfolding for days, continued, taking up several columns of the newspaper. *Wow,* I thought to myself, *What is this world coming to?*

I realized that the soldiers of truth that had been waging war on the battlefield of my mind had somehow challenged my worldview.

We finally arrived at the conference, where a couple of thousand people were waiting in a beautiful sanctuary complete with deeply padded chairs. An anointed worship team led us in adoration to the Lord, their voices mixed to perfection on a $30,000 soundboard and distributed to us through a state-of-the-art sound system.

Soon it was my turn to speak. "The world is getting darker and darker as we progress through these Last Days," I proclaimed. But something didn't seem right about that statement anymore. I struggled in my soul, feeling like I was being dishonest with the congregation. It was then I realized that the soldiers of truth that had been waging war on the battlefield of my mind had somehow challenged my worldview.

I began to question reality and wonder where I had picked up these negative mindsets while living in a level of luxury that kings hadn't known a mere century ago.

Dark Glasses

As I pondered these things, I came to recognize that I was born into a world darkened in understanding. Although I was enlightened to the truth of salvation by faith, I had somehow chosen to leave the dark glasses of doubt on when viewing the Lord's parish, the world that He loved so much. After all, such sunglasses were in vogue—everybody was wearing them, and I didn't want the Christian crowd to reject me.

I have since come to recognize that bad news sells. The average person today hears more negative reports in one week than someone just 50 years ago would have heard in his or her lifetime.

The average person today hears more negative reports in one week than someone just 50 years ago would have heard in his or her lifetime.

I also began to understand that the world has satisfied its appetite for bad news by developing tracking systems that report what is wrong in the world instead of what is right. For example, we track the unemployment rate, not the employment rate. Think about the mindset that develops from focusing on the fact that 12 percent of our nation's workforce is unemployed instead of the fact that 88 percent of Americans are working. So many statistics are designed to gauge what's wrong with humanity instead of what is right.

Bad news is so popular that the media has even figured out a way to negatively report good news. Gas prices are a great example of this. When the average price of gas rose to more than $2 a gallon in June 2008, the news reports spoke of the evils of hyperinflation. Later, when the average prices dropped to an average of $1.61 per gallon in December, the media headlines thundered, "The economic ills of deflation."

I am not trying to bury my head in the sand and pretend there are no serious problems in the world. Nor am I advocating living in a fantasy world of denial and calling it faith. But I will not relegate my worldview to lies so that I can somehow rejoice over the fulfillment of some "end time" verse in the Bible. God wants us to embrace the truth, not popular opinion.

I will not relegate my worldview to lies so that I can somehow rejoice over the fulfillment of some "end time" verse in the Bible. God wants us to embrace the truth, not popular opinion.

Good News Is Hard to Believe

There has been so much good news on this planet in the last 100 years that it is hard to comprehend why it isn't on the front page of every newspaper in the country. Thankfully, Stephen Moore and Julian L. Simon have gone through the trouble to compile many of these neglected facts in one volume called *It's Getting Better All the Time: 100 Greatest Trends of the Last 100 Years.* I'd like to share just a sampling of their findings with you here.

Health

Diseases that for decades wiped out entire civilizations have been completely eradicated from the globe. Smallpox, polio, tuberculosis and leprosy are ancient history lessons studied in textbooks read by elementary school children.

For much of human history, the average life expectancy of a person used to be between 20 to 30 years; but by 2003, the average person worldwide lived to be nearly 67 years old, and life expectancy is still rising.[2] Even in Africa, the poorest continent in the world, it has increased to 46 years old.[3]

For much of human history, the average life expectancy of a person used to be between 20 to 30 years.

But wait; there is more good news. Not only are people living longer today, but they are also healthier in their old age. People get sick much later in life. For example, people contract heart disease at least nine years later than they did just a century ago. Respiratory diseases have been delayed an average of 11 years and cancer eight years.[4]

Before industrialization, at least one out of every five children died before reaching his or her first birthday, but by 2003, the worldwide infant mortality rate had dropped by nearly 75 percent to 1 in every 17 children.[5]

Before industrialization, at least one out of every five children died before reaching his or her first birthday.

While we are on the subject of health, let's talk about smoking. In 1965, approximately one of every two people smoked in America. By the year 2006, that number dropped to about one in every five people.[6] In other words, in the last 40 years or so, nearly 64 million people have quit smoking in the U.S. alone!

Let's examine a few more indicators suggesting that the world is improving rather than digressing.

Over the 25-year period beginning in 1962 and ending in 1987, smog levels fell by more than half.

Pollution

In 1968, doomsayer Paul Ehrlich wrote in his book *The Population Bomb* that "smog disasters" might kill 200,000 people in New York and Los Angeles alone by 1973.[7] The reality is that air pollution in American cities has been falling for at least the past three decades. Favorable urban air quality trends have not been confined to just a handful of cities either. Over the 25-year period beginning in 1962 and ending in 1987, smog levels fell by more than half.[8]

Not only is air quality improving drastically, water quality is also improving. According to the Pacific Research Institutes *Index of Leading Environmental Indicators,* in 1972 only 36 percent of U.S. lakes were usable for fishing and swimming. By 1994, that number rose to 91 percent![9]

The percentage of water sources that were judged to be poor or severe by the Council on Environmental Quality fell from 30 percent in 1961 to less than 5 percent today.[10]

Poverty

The average person has never been better fed than they are today. Between 1961 and 2002, the world's average daily food supply increased by 24 percent (38 percent in developing nations) per person. Chronic undernourishment in developing nations declined from 37 percent to 17 percent of their population in that same period.[11]

Between 1961 and 2002, the world's average daily food supply increased by 24 percent per person.

Since 1950, greater agricultural productivity and international trade has caused inflation-adjusted prices of food commodities to decline by 75 percent. At the same time, access to safe water and sanitation has increased dramatically.[12]

Abortion

In spite of all the "pro-choice" media pressure leveled at society, abortion rates are tumbling. According to the Guttmacher Institute's 2005 survey of abortion providers, the abortion rate declined 25 percent during the last 15 years in the United States.[13] That equates to 400,000 fewer babies aborted in America alone in 2005 than there were in 1990. The good news is that the abortion rate is still dropping drastically!

There were 400,000 fewer babies aborted in America in 2005 than there were in 1990.

Let me make it clear that abortion is still the most serious crime ever committed against humanity, and millions of children are still being aborted here and abroad. We need to continue the struggle for the unborn until abortion is ancient history like smallpox. But what I am pointing out is that we can see clear movement in that direction.

More people lived on the earth in this last century than have been born in all of previous history combined!

Population Growth

Decreasing abortion rates, longer life expectancy, reduced infant deaths, major decreases in starvation, and the overall improving state of the planet have resulted in the world's population growing quite dramatically. At the turn of the twentieth century, for example, the population of the earth was about 1.6 billion. Today there are more then 6.7 billion people gracing this planet! More people lived on the earth in this last century than have been born in all of previous history combined! Experts say that by 2050 there will be 9 billion people living on this planet.[14] What's exciting about this is that behind every number is a person made in God's image.

Let's look at some other areas of social and moral progress.

Civil Rights

When we think of the oppression of women in countries like Afghanistan, we often forget that until August 26, 1920, women in America could not even vote! After thousands of years of oppression and domination by men, women are finally winning back their God-given place in society. When God created mankind, both male and female, He commissioned them both to take dominion over the planet (see Genesis 1:26-28). Men were never given authority over women until the Fall in the Garden. Contrary to popular opinion, male domination was part of the curse, not the original order of creation (see Genesis 3:16)! Jesus was crucified to deliver all of creation from the curse. Two thousand years later, women all over the world are beginning to experience the freedom that their Savior purchased for them on the cross. Women are finding their way into the marketplace in record numbers. They are emerging as incredible leaders in business, education, politics and every walk of life and field of employment. Heck, even the Body of Christ is realizing our need for female leadership and commissioning women to help govern our churches. Go, ladies!

> **Women are finding their way into the marketplace in record numbers.**

A discussion about American civil rights wouldn't be complete without recounting the African-American struggle for freedom and equality. From 1654 until 1863, slavery was legal within the boundaries of much of the present United States. It was only after the bloodiest war in U.S. history that Abraham Lincoln's Emancipation Proclamation freed black people from slavery, though the struggle for freedom went on long after the legal battle was won. The Fifteenth Amendment to the Constitution granted African-American men the right to vote by declaring that the "right of citizens of the United States to vote shall not be denied or abridged by the United States or by any state on account of race, color, or previous condition of servitude." Although ratified on February 3, 1870, the promise of the Fifteenth Amendment would not be fully realized for almost a century.

Again, the civil rights movement of the sixties, stimulated by Rosa Parks and led by Dr. Martin Luther King, continued the struggle of equality for African-American citizens. Dr. King gave his life fighting for equal rights for people of all colors. Watching President Obama take the oath of the highest office in our land had to be the ultimate climax in African-American history so far. Even if you didn't vote for him, you can still feel a sense of poetic justice in his presidency.

Freedom to Vote

Since the women's rights movement and the civil rights movement, most Americans take the right to vote for granted. But in 1900, no country had universal suffrage (the right for all its adult citizens to vote) and only 12.4 percent of the world's population had even limited suffrage. Today, 44.1 percent of the world's population lives in nations deemed free by Freedom House and another 18.6 percent in nations deemed partly free.[15]

Spiritual Hunger

Throughout this chapter we have discussed just a little bit of the good news taking place in our world today and have yet to even touch on the positive spiritual movements of our times. Did you know that more people are finding Christ today than any time in human history? Do you realize that many places once dominated by atheism, Islam and Buddhism are now experiencing incredible revivals? The intense spiritual hunger in China, Africa and Russia, for example, is causing unprecedented revival. In our own movement, we literally see hundreds of healings, miracles, salvations and divine interventions of God every month.

Why Are Things Getting Worse?

So why are people convinced that the world is eroding rather than evolving? Well, first you have to find out who is carrying this negative message. Do you suppose that any open-minded person actually believes the world is getting worse for women? How about for African Americans? How would they answer this question: "Is your race worse off today then it was a hundred years ago?" Are the Russians better off today than they were under communism? Or was the world a better place under the tyranny of Hitler, Stalin and Saddam Hussein?

Do you suppose that any open-minded person actually believes the world is getting worse for women?

If the believers who are least in the kingdom of God are superior to the greatest prophet (John the Baptist) who ever lived under the Old Covenant, then at least we know that folks who receive Christ today are better off than they were in ancient times (see Matthew 11:11). And if Christ died to disarm the devil and gave all authority to His church, then we would have to conclude that the world is better off than it was before Christ's victory on the cross (see Colossians 2:13-15; Ephesians 1:18-23).

You're Missing the Point!

"All right," you say, "I concede. But you are ignoring the major sin issues of our time. How about murder, homosexuality, the cults and the occult? Aren't they taking over our world?" Well, think about it for a minute. The first murder took place with only four people on the planet. So when Cain killed Abel, the murder rate instantly rose to 25 percent. And contrary to popular opinion, homosexuality didn't begin in San Francisco; it is reported in the Bible. It was so prevalent that we get one of our names for sexual perversion from a biblical town (Sodom).

Do you believe that political corruption was initiated at Watergate? Have you ever read the story of David's (the man after God's own heart) adulterous relationship with Bath-sheba and murder of Uriah, her husband? Do you realize that 80 percent of all of Israel's kings listed in the Bible were wicked?

Do you think that false religions began with the New Age movement? Have you not read all the accounts of the worship of Baal and the children that were sacrificed on his altars in the Old Testament? Are you aware that the psychics of today were the satraps of Daniel's day? Do you believe that Greek mythology is any less destructive than Mormonism, Jehovah's Witnesses or Islam? Maybe the good old days were not quite as wonderful as we like to recount them.

The World Is a More Dangerous Place Today

"Well, okay, but isn't it true that with the invention of the atomic bomb, the world is a much more dangerous place?" The answer to that question is yes . . . and no. Of course, even an idiot has to acknowledge that it's the first time in history that mankind literally has the capacity to destroy the planet. If some nut starts a nuclear war, all the facts in this chapter *could* become instantly irrelevant.

On the other hand, for centuries violent dictators have ravaged weaker countries, pillaging their people and destroying their cities. Tyrants like Alexander the Great, Julius Caesar,

Adolph Hitler, Napoleon of France, Joseph Stalin, Vladimir Lenin and Genghis Khan were determined to rule the world by crushing their opposition with their military might. These men ruled their empires with an iron fist, committing unimaginable atrocities against their enemies and often terrorizing their own citizens.

But strangely, since the invention of the atomic bomb and the demonstration of its destructive ability, tyrants have been kept in check, knowing that their violent acts of aggression could very well result in their country being blown off the map. And even if the oppressor has nuclear weapons, attacking another nation protected by the same arsenal is a lose-lose situation. When the battle is over and the mushroom clouds finally dissipate, there is nothing left to rule.

After Adolph Hitler tried to conquer the world, the nations were motivated to work together to stop tyrants and promote world peace. The United Nations was founded in 1946 on the premise of ensuring international security and protecting human rights. Although this young organization has often not fulfilled its professed mission very well (i.e., in Rwanda, where U.N. peacekeeping forces pulled out of the country during the genocide, allowing a million people to be slaughtered in three months), it is a huge step forward in the process of a better and safer world.

Antichrist Is Coming!

Even as I write this chapter, I am aware that there are a large number of Christians convinced that any form of cooperative globalization is the beginning of the Antichrist's one-world government, which will be followed by the Mark of the Beast and climax in the battle of Armageddon. Are you aware that the idea of the Antichrist developing a one-world government is basically being taught on the basis of three Scripture passages? Here they are:

In that you saw the feet and toes, partly of potter's clay and partly of iron, it will be a divided kingdom; but it will have in it the toughness of iron, inasmuch as you saw the iron mixed with common clay. As the toes of the feet were partly of iron and partly of pottery, so some of the kingdom will be strong and part of it will be brittle (Daniel 2:41-42).

I approached one of those who were standing by and began asking him the exact meaning of all this. So he told me and made known to me the interpretation of these things: "These great beasts, which are four in number, are four kings who will arise from the earth. But the saints of the Highest One will receive the kingdom and possess the kingdom forever, for all ages to come." Then I desired to know the exact meaning of the fourth beast, which was different from all the others, exceedingly dreadful, with its teeth of iron and its claws of bronze, and which devoured, crushed and trampled down the remainder with its feet, and the meaning of the ten horns that were on its head and the other horn which came up, and before which three of them fell, namely, that horn which had eyes and a mouth uttering great boasts and which was larger in appearance than its associates. I kept looking, and that horn was waging war with the saints and overpowering them until the Ancient of Days came and judgment was passed in favor of the saints of the Highest One, and the time arrived when the saints took possession of the kingdom. Thus he said: "The fourth beast will be a fourth kingdom on the earth, which will be different from all the other kingdoms and will devour the whole earth and tread it down and crush it. As for the ten horns, out of this kingdom ten kings will arise; and another will arise after them, and he will be different from the previous ones and will subdue three kings. He will speak out against the Most High and wear down the saints of the Highest One, and he will intend to make alterations in times and in law; and they will be given into his hand for a time, times, and half a time" (Daniel 7:16-25).

And the dragon stood on the sand of the seashore. Then I saw a beast coming up out of the sea, having ten horns and seven heads, and on his horns were ten diadems, and on his heads were blasphemous names. . . . It was also given to him to make war with the saints and to overcome them, and authority over every tribe and people and tongue and nation was given to him (Revelation 13:1,7).

Did you find the Antichrist's one-world government in these passages? Well, apparently you should have, because these are the main Scriptures that are causing thousands of Christians to resist nations working together for the common good of the global population. Is it just me, or do you think that someone would have to have a pretty good imagination (or preconceived idea) to get a one-world Antichrist government out of these Scriptures? I have a struggle with believers who read their ideas into the Scriptures, especially in a way that undermines the Great Commission and subverts the Lord's Prayer.

The World Is Damned

Many Christians have developed a "damned if you do and damned if you don't" theological worldview. They are so convinced that things "must get worse" for Jesus to return that they have become marooned on a small island, lost somewhere between "You will be hearing of wars and rumors of wars" (Matthew 24:6) and "while they are saying, 'Peace and safety!' then destruction will come upon them suddenly" (1 Thessalonians 5:3). If these two Scriptures make up your entire eschatological paradigm, then you basically have two boxes to put all your world news in: Bad news goes into the "Everything needs to get worse" box, and good news gets sorted into the "If things look good, destruction is near" box.

Many Christians have developed a "damned if you do and damned if you don't" theological worldview.

How do you have any faith for the restoration of nations (see Isaiah 61:4), making disciples of *all* nations (see Matthew 28:19), destroying the works of the devil (see 1 John 3:8) and doing greater works (miracles) than Jesus did if you only embrace a few portions of Scripture as the full counsel of God?

Final Thoughts

As I pointed out in the previous chapter, I am not claiming to have all the answers. I certainly do not. But I have found that people who think they have all the answers usually have misunderstood the questions. The challenges we face today are complex, and they won't ever be solved by one person or answered in a single book.

> I have found that people who think
> they have all the answers usually have
> misunderstood the questions.

However, I believe wisdom comes as we define reality. Pilate asked Jesus, "What is truth?" (John 18:38). He wasn't asking Jesus, "What does the Bible say?" No, the Greek word for "truth" here means "real." Pilate was literally asking Jesus, "What is real?" You can't define reality until you have questioned it!

> You can't define reality until you
> have questioned it!

I must admit that in these critical days in which we live, I have often found myself asking Jesus the same question Pilate asked when he was making the most important decision of his life (whether or not he should crucify Christ). Pilate finally got it right, but it was too late. The best he could do was wash his hands of the situation (see Matthew 27:24).

> During the American Civil War,
> many very devout Christians fought for
> (in favor of) slavery.

During the American Civil War, many very devout Christians fought *for* (in favor of) slavery. These believers took Scriptures like Paul's letter to the Colossians to mean they had the God-given right to enslave people:

> Slaves, in all things obey those who are your masters on earth, not with external service, as those who merely please men, but with sincerity of heart, fearing the Lord (Colossians 3:22).

> Masters, grant to your slaves justice and fairness, knowing that you too have a Master in heaven (Colossians 4:1).

Sadly, they got it wrong, and 620,000 people died in a Civil War to set things right.

My Vision

I was lying on the floor of our prayer house in 2004, seeking God, when suddenly I was taken up in a vision that thrust me 100 years into the future. I found myself standing next to an old man in the living room of a huge, ornate mansion. I could see him perfectly, but he couldn't see me. It felt like it was Thanksgiving or something—the home was filled with the smells of pies baking in the oven, and the excitement of a large family gathering was in the air. The adults were talking and laughing as the kids played. The elderly gentleman was encircled with several generations of family, all listening intently as he exuberantly told them stories, musing over the past as old men often do. Then something happened. His tone changed and his face grew serious, as if he was about to share something of great importance with them. Tears formed in his eyes as he looked off into the distance, like he was trying to recall some ancient secret told to him long ago. The entire room grew silent and more people gathered, leaning in to hear every word.

He began to speak to them about their noble roots and their royal heritage, staring into the eyes of each one as if he was looking for greatness in their souls. He spoke of the great price their forefathers had paid to obtain such favor, wealth and influence from God and man. But it was what he did next that stunned me. He pointed to a majestic stone fireplace that rose about 30 feet to a vaulted ceiling. I looked over toward the fireplace mantle where a large, beautiful artist's portrait of Kathy and me hung. I was breathless as he finished his exhortation: "All this began with your great-great-great-grandmother and -grandfather!"

I instantly came out of the vision, struggling to gather my thoughts. Next I heard a thundering voice speak to my spirit: "Your children's children's children are depending on you leaving them a world in revival. You are no longer to live for a ministry. From this day forward, you are to live to leave a legacy!"

If we misinterpret God's heart for the future, it will be our children's children's children who will pay the greatest price for our mistake. If we get this right, we could be the catalyst to the greatest revival in the history of the world.

There is a Heavy Rain coming that is about to saturate the entire planet. What will it look like when God pours His Spirit out on all flesh? This entire book has been dedicated to seeing and taking hold of God's vision for the future. We can't afford to get this wrong. If we misinterpret God's heart for the future, it will be our children's children's children who will pay the greatest price for our mistake. On the other hand, if we get this right, we could be the catalyst to the greatest revival in the history of the world. LET IT RAIN!

Notes

1. Bob Thiele and George David Weiss, "What a Wonderful World," performed by Louis Armstrong, © 1967 ABC Records.
2. Indur Goklany, *The Improving State of the World: Why We're Living Longer, Healthier, More Comfortable Lives on a Cleaner Planet* (Washington, DC: The Cato Institute, 2007), p. 31.
3. Ibid., p. 69.
4. Ibid., p. 40.
5. Ibid., p. 27.
6. "Cigarette Smoking Among Adults—United States, 2006," *Morbidity and Mortality Weekly Report,* Centers for Disease Control and Prevention, November 7, 2007. http://www.cdc.gov/mmwr/preview/mmwrhtml/mm5644a2.htm#fig.
7. Stephen Moore and Julian L. Simon, *It's Getting Better All the Time: 100 Greatest Trends of the Last 100 Years* (Washington, DC: The Cato Institute, 2000), p. 186.
8. Ibid.
9. Ibid., p. 188.
10. Ibid.
11. Goklany, *The Improving State of the World,* p. 21.
12. Ibid., pp. 43-44.
13. Rachel K. Jones, Mia R.S. Zolna, Stanley K. Henshaw and Lawrence B. Finer, "Abortion in the United States: Incidence and Access to Services, 2005," Guttmacher Institute, vol. 40, no. 1, March 2008. www.guttmacher.org/pubs/journals/4000608.pdf.
14. "World Population: 1950-2050," U.S. Census Bureau, International Data Base, June 2010. http://www.census.gov/ipc/www/idb/worldpopgraph.php.
15. Goklany, *The Improving State of the World,* pp. 47-49.

About the Author

Kris Vallotton is the author of several books and a much-sought-after international conference speaker. Kris has a passion to see people's lives transformed and to be a catalyst to world transformation.

In 1998, Kris Vallotton co-founded the Bethel School of Supernatural Ministry in Redding, California, which has grown to more than 1,900 full-time students. Kris is the senior associate leader at Bethel Church and has been a part of Bill Johnson's apostolic team for more than three decades.

Kris is also the founder and CEO of Moral Revolution, an organization dedicated to a worldwide sexual reformation.

Kris and his wife, Kathy, have been happily married for more than 38 years. They have four children and eight grandchildren.

For more information, please visit
www.kvministries.com

OTHER BOOKS AND MESSAGES
BY KRIS VALLOTTON

Books

Developing a Supernatural Lifestyle
The Supernatural Ways of Royalty
Basic Training for the Supernatural Ways of Royalty
Basic Training for the Prophetic Ministry
Moral Revolution

Messages

Casting Vision, Catching Hearts
Developing a Legacy
Is Your House Haunted?
Fighting for Your Place in History
For the Love of God
From Paupers to Princes
Fear Is Not Your Friend
From the Pool to the River
Mercy Triumphs over Judgment
Leadership for an Epoch Season 1, 2 & 3
The Tipping Point
Living from Eternity

These and many other titles are available at
www.kvministries.com